*Old Books
in the
Old World*

OLD BOOKS
IN THE
OLD WORLD

Reminiscences of Book Buying Abroad

by Leona Rostenberg
& Madeleine B. Stern

1996
Oak Knoll Press
New Castle, Delaware

First published in 1996 by

OAK KNOLL PRESS

414 Delaware Street, New Castle, DE 19720, U.S.A.

Trade edition: ISBN 1-884718-18-3
Limited edition: ISBN 1-884718-21-3

Book design, editing and production by
Joel Friedlander Publishing Services

Manufactured in the United States of America

Distributed by Lyons & Burford, Publishers
31 West 21 Street, New York, NY 10010

Library of Congress Cataloging in Publication Data

Rostenberg, Leona.
  Old books in the old world : reminiscences of book buying
abroad / by Leona Rostenberg & Madeleine B. Stern.
    p. cm.
  Includes index.
  ISBN 1-884718-18-3 (alk. paper)
  1. Rostenberg, Leona. 2. Stern, Madeleine B.,
3. Antiquarian booksellers—New York (N.Y.)—Biography. 4. Book
collectors—New York (N.Y.)—Biography. 5. Books—Europe,
Western—Purchasing—History—20th century. 6. Antiquarian
booksellers—Europe, Western—History—20th century. I. Stern,
Madeleine B.,   II. Title.
Z473.R77R66   1996
381'.45002'092—dc20   95-51068
                                          CIP

CONTENTS

List of Illustrations . . . *vi*

Authors' Note. . . *vii*

Introduction . . . *1*

1947: London — Cambridge — Paris — Strasbourg —
Basle — The Hague . . . *17*

1948: London — Oxford . . . *35*

1949: London . . . *51*

1951: London — Oxford — Cambridge —
Canterbury . . . *65*

1952: London — Paris . . . *79*

1953: Paris — London . . . *91*

1954: London — Vienna — Paris . . . *105*

1955: The Hague — Paris — London — Provinces . . . *121*

1956: The Hague — Venice — Florence — Milan —
Paris — London . . . *135*

1957: The Hague — Brussels — Basle — Zurich —
Geneva — Milan — Paris . . . *151*

Index . . . *165*

ILLUSTRATIONS

L. and M. diary entries . . . *viii*

Travel announcement . . . 3

Oxford Street in August 1949 . . . 4

L. at Joseph's . . . 8

L. in her office . . . 12

Bound for the hunt on the *Veendam*, 1947 . . . 18

Thorp's, Berkeley Street, London, August 1947 . . . 20

L. at McLeish, London, 1947 . . . 21

E.P. Goldschmidt . . . 22

"Work or Want," Billboard, London, 1947 . . . 25

Percy Dobell, Mt. Ephraim Road, Tunbridge Wells, 1947 . . . 26

Bowes & Bowes, Trinity Street, Cambridge, 1947 . . . 27

L. at Farringdon Street Market, August 1947 . . . 29

Brunier's, 1947 . . . 30

Martinus Nijhoff, The Hague, September 18, 1947 . . . 33

L. at Traylen's, Guildford, September 1948 . . . 45

Travel announcement, 1951 . . . 66

M. and L. aboard the *Nieuw Amsterdam*, 1951 . . . 66

Travel announcement, 1953 . . . 92

M. and L. in the office, 1953 . . . 102

L. and Winifred Myers at Strawberry Hill, 1954 . . . 107

ILAB Congress, Vienna, 1954 . . . 113

M. and L. at National Bibliothek Prunksaal, Vienna, 1954 . . . 115

Place cards at ILAB banquet . . . 116

Ludwig Rosenthal's, Hilversum, The Netherlands, July 1955 . . . 123

Emily Driscoll and L. in Tuileries Gardens, July 1955 . . . 127

M. and Nat Ladden, Hyde Park, July 1955 . . . 128

M., Ernest and Gertrude Weil, July 16, 1955 . . . 129

M. at Exeter . . . 133

ILAB Farewell Dinner program, London, 1956 . . . 147

Haus der Bücher (Erasmushaus), Basle, 1957 . . . 154

*To retain the spontaneity and informality
of the originals, extracts from our journals and letters
have been transcribed exactly as they were written,
often in the heat of the moment.*

Fifty years later, we dedicate this book to each other.

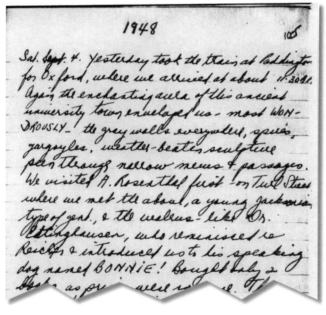

Leona Rostenberg diary entry, August 5, 1949

Madeleine B. Stern diary entry, September 4, 1948

INTRODUCTION

In that vanished world between 1947 and 1957 when we first journeyed abroad in search of antiquarian books, certain conditions prevailed that had long-lasting effects. That decade determined to a large extent the development both of our business and of our way of life.

The transatlantic voyage with which most of those journeys began was itself a determining factor. Its length, anywhere from 7 to 10 days, influenced both the length and the nature of our stay abroad. Between Hoboken, NJ, and Southampton, England, no shuttle trip was available. If our voyage lasted a week or more, naturally our European stay would last a month or more. We did not fly over in 7 hours to negotiate a sale, view a collection, or attend an auction. And when, in 1954, we did begin to fly, we were still 17 hours in the air with a stopover on Cape Breton Island. Hence, we remained abroad long enough to visit dozens of dealers, to walk the cobbled streets and mews and lanes, to savor the nature of the country as well as the contents of its bookshops. In addition, between 1947 and 1957, only the most intrepid dealers ventured abroad. There were so few booksellers traveling overseas that the British passport control recognized us from one year to the next!

Since our stays abroad were not only uncommon but extended, we kept records of them. Clifford Maggs, reviewing *Old & Rare* for the *Antiquarian Book Monthly Review*, wrote: "There is a freshness in the impressions recorded that springs from the use of diaries and letters." Those diaries and letters, kept in the course of a decade's European bookbuying, are all here. They were written because, between 1947 and 1957, we had family eager to follow our itineraries and enjoy the vicarious delights of our experiences. One year only is unrepresented in the record. In 1950 the illness and subsequent death of Leona's father kept us close to home.

Now, 40 years after they were read by their original audience, the letters and journals are published for a larger readership who will find, restored to life against the forgotten background of postwar Europe, the books we found, the ghostly booksellers we visited, and the two of us as we began our bookselling careers.

We had embarked upon the business of buying and selling antiquarian books because we were what we were. And we were what we were because of our backgrounds, our families, our education. All these molded our interests, shaped our characters, and led us first into partnership and then into the adventure of bookbuying abroad.

As undergraduates, we honed our individual fascinations — Leona in history at New York University, Madeleine in literature at Barnard. As graduate students at Columbia, we developed those fascinations into addictions. There Leona began her investigation of the 16th-century printer-publisher's influence upon history and society, and Madeleine began to trace the literary treatment of historical characters. Both tasks exposed them to rare books, but it was Leona who, during her months in the library of the University of Strasbourg, actually became the familiar of rare books. Subsequently she spent a five-year apprenticeship working in New York for a refugee dealer from Austria, Herbert Reichner, who brought to this country and transmitted to her an in-depth knowledge of early continental books.

The two of us had been friends long before we became business partners. The friendship rendered the partnership inevitable. In 1944, Leona Rostenberg issued announcements that she had entered the rare book business, operating from her home. Six months later, on April 10, 1945, Madeleine, having completed a Guggenheim Fellowship for a biography of Louisa May Alcott and resigned from the teaching of English, joined her as partner.

During the next two years, Madeleine's role was as much that of student as partner, since it was Leona rather than Madeleine who had an already amazing grasp of the old and the rare. Together they issued their first two catalogues: the first on "The History of the Book" in 1946, the second on "The House of Elzevier" in 1947. By July 29 of that year, when the *Veendam* sailed from its pier in Hoboken, NJ, the two proprietors of Leona Rostenberg Rare Books were on board, ready to apply what they had learned, eager to fill empty shelves in some imaginary open shop, hoping to match their wits with those of dealers who were as yet merely names on rare book catalogues.

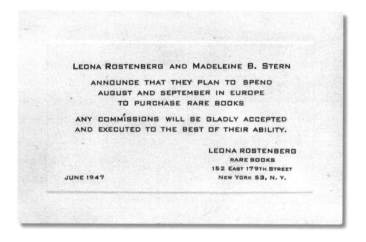

LEONA ROSTENBERG AND MADELEINE B. STERN

ANNOUNCE THAT THEY PLAN TO SPEND
AUGUST AND SEPTEMBER IN EUROPE
TO PURCHASE RARE BOOKS

ANY COMMISSIONS WILL BE GLADLY ACCEPTED
AND EXECUTED TO THE BEST OF THEIR ABILITY.

LEONA ROSTENBERG
RARE BOOKS
152 EAST 179TH STREET
JUNE 1947   NEW YORK 53, N. Y.

Secure in the indulgences of home, we were far less ready, and indeed almost totally unprepared, to face the post-war horrors of England and the repercussions of the Holocaust on the continent. As far as we could observe, the Battle of Britain was still being waged. Departing a customs house established in a temporary shed at Southampton, we saw surrounding us all the way to London vestiges of war — bombed buildings, the mute evidence of shells, twisted iron work, windowless structures open to the elements. In 1948, when we purchased a little guidebook to London, we saw every other place marked with an asterisk indicating it had been closed because of war damage. In some cases, we would learn, the war damage would never be effaced, as in the case of one of our British dealers, Francis Norman, whom "the blitz had estranged from life."* In other cases there would be gradual improvement which we would observe from year to year.

Oxford Street in August 1949

Accompanying the exterior horrors were the rigidities and austerities imposed in Britain by strict post-war regulations. Ration books and queues had become, it seemed, a continuing way of life. The substitution of horse and whalemeat for beef seemed particularly devastating to these two spoiled Americans who eventually brought a Sterno with them and secretively cooked Franco-American spaghetti in their room at the Hotel Cumberland. Restrictions were especially stiff regarding expenditure for food. One was not permitted to spend more than a certain amount for any dinner, and one night when we each ordered a custard, we were informed that we might spend only 35 cents more. Two custards would have come to 40 cents — so we had to share one!

Gradually, as we returned, year after year, we saw the rigidities loosen, the good things of life return to British tables, the lights come on in England. Some of the bombed spots were rebuilt or covered with false fronts; by 1952 Big Ben and Whitehall were bathed in light for the Festival of Britain; and all London seemed "sunlit by day & floodlit by night." Tempers improved and so did the food: eggs once a week, oranges for sale on the barrows, paper napkins at table. By

---

*All quotations in the Introduction are from the text that follows.

1954, "life is easy once again," and by 1956 at the International Congress, the Farewell Banquet would be a repast of sherry turtle soup, sole, filet mignon, and Baked Alaska. We two no longer yearned to return home, but rather felt at home abroad.

British attitude toward America changed too during those years. In 1947 America was still the promised land. "All Europe," we wrote, "wants to get to America." The Rosenberg case, the Communist threat, the shifting political patterns of Europe altered that early faith and dimmed the gratitude. By 1955, Yankees were invited to go home. What did not seem to change was the British love of pageantry — a scarlet thread that persisted through the years of drabness.

Across the Channel, the postwar horrors that struck us most poignantly were less external than internal. Primarily they were the effects of that part of the war known as the Holocaust. The decayed buildings, the pointed tommy guns, the military police of occupied Vienna somehow affected us less than the people we encountered in the Netherlands. "We have shed more tears in Holland," we wrote, "than anywhere else." We met only the survivors of course — one of them Jelle Menage who, because he had helped seven Jews hide during the Occupation, had been forced to stand naked at attention in a concentration camp from 4 a.m. to 9 p.m. Among the dealers who had survived the Occupation, detention, or the life of the Underground were Menno Hertzberger and Hilde Rosenthal. Survivors extraordinary, both of them, who somehow rebuilt their lives and their book businesses from the ruins. We had met others too, in other countries — the refugee Baer in a shabby London flat; and, in his "turreted villa" outside Paris, Michel Bernstein who had been one of the French Resistance and lived underground during the war. But nowhere did we feel the effects of the Nazi horror so keenly as in the Netherlands.

And so we sensed if not experienced the effects of war and persecution. We had seen the British attempt a rehabilitation by means of rigidity and austerity; we had seen the French approach the peace by maneuverings in a black market. We had seen the devastation in the streets and the grief of many who survived to walk those streets.

On nearly every street in Paris a house bore a memorial plaque honoring a Frenchman who had defied German authority and been gunned down.

But all this was for us a kind of lagniappe. This was not what we had come for. We had come to buy books and to meet the booksellers whose catalogues we had studied. We had come to explore the bookshops and *librairies* and *libreria,* from "the glorious heights" of Berkeley Square to "the lowly depths of a cellar off Holborn Place," from the rue Bonaparte to the Boulevard St. Germain, from the Via Borgonuovo to the Via Montebello.

The decade from 1947 to 1957 was a halcyon time for such a purpose. The truly great dealers — those who valued knowledge above money and substance above glitter — were still alive, still active. We were privileged to have met them and dealt with them during those years — along with the lesser, colorful, Dickensian characters who filled the bibliopolic ranks and appeared from time to time in our journals. They were our dramatis personae against the background of the post-war years. They filled our shelves at the same time that they planted themselves in our memories.

Among our greats, E. P. Goldschmidt must rank first — the scholar-bookseller of Old Bond Street who transported us back to the Renaissance and sent us on our way treading on air. For us he remains the patriarch of a trade he helped transform into a profession. He enlightened us with little-known facts about an early binding motif or a monastery find, but mostly he admitted us to a world inhabited by a Grolier or a Dibdin, where we came to feel at home.

Not far removed from Goldschmidt's pedestal were other greats from whom we bought in London: Goldschmidt's onetime partner Ernest Weil, who combined books — mostly scientific rarities — with comfortable gossip and high tea; Irving Davis, the pipe-sucking Italianate Englishman whose mind was as crowded with unusual facts as his warehouse was with unusual tracts; Ted Dring of the great house of Quaritch; Clifford Maggs of Berkeley Square, who measured us with an appraising eye as he watched us enter our purchases in our ledger at the Dickens table.

And then there were our continental greats whose habits and business methods might differ from the British variety, but whose knowledge was as deep and whose perception was as sharp. On the rue de Tournon, when we first began our Parisian scouting, Lucien Scheler, distinguished poet-scholar, held sway, mildly suggesting, elucidating, enlightening, before he passed the torch to his successor. Indeed it was he who telephoned to Michel Bernstein arranging an appointment that would lead to annual visits with the prime dealer in political theory, the dealer who had amassed from journeys to provincial abbeys and private estates the books and pamphlets that reflected France's changing government from the 16th to the 19th century.

In the Netherlands, another great dealer, Hilde Rosenthal, who succeeded to the firm of Ludwig Rosenthal, was less specialized than our French eminents. At her establishment in Hilversum one could spend days plowing through fiches, books, pamphlets that ranged from a 16th-century life of Tamerlane the Great to the *North Georgia Gazette* of 1821. Fortified by a Rosenthal lunch, a visiting dealer could pluck from the Rosenthal stock the plums of 5 centuries.

Against a different background, another great dealer, Cesare Olschki, flourished on the Lungarno of Florence. Outside were the Tuscan hills; inside, a stock that encompassed the philosophy and literature, the art and romance of many different worlds. We had studied Italian under the guidance of the super-grammatical Signorina Snyder in preparation for our first book-buying venture in Italy. As a result, we could barely make ourselves understood. Fortunately, Signor Olschki was multilingual, and thanks to his kindness and consideration, we were able to purchase, after two days on the Via Vente Settembre, 163 books, and eventually from our Florentine forays we would be able to assemble an entire Medici collection.

Our bibliopolic cast of characters between 1947 and 1957 included many lesser lights as well. They too should be remembered, if not for the books we bought from them, then for their own peculiar natures and eccentricities. They were all colorful individuals who enriched the fabric of the book trade during post-war years.

In our minds and in our journals, the Dickensian Miss Fanny Hamel of Grafton's still wears her broad-brimmed hat, still eyes us cautiously, still berates the burden of consular invoices and scolds her staff mercilessly on Great Russell Street. On Charing Cross Road, Jack Joseph still sports his bowler and natty vest and escorts us to his cellar as he inveighs about the government. In Hampstead, Francis Norman is forever shrouded in the debris of a cluttered shop that once yielded us a pearl. Farther afield, in Newbury, H. W. Edwards, "6 generations of Cockney behind him," overflows with forthright opinions designed to shock and stimulate at once.

L. at Josephs's

Bibliopolic birds of strange plumage flew on the continent too. We think of the obese and asthmatic Herr Hinterberger in Vienna, as agile as he was rotund, equipped with a list of books on any subject we could suggest. In Geneva we think of the charming and generous Paul Bader who preferred fishing to bookselling, but who sold us books nonetheless and left notes for us under his shop door. In Paris there were perhaps more colorful dealers than anywhere else. Pierre Lambert, almost always *en vacance*, discusses the grave of his adored Huysmans and sells us books on the cash-and-carry plan. Monsieur Thiebaud fixes his foxy blue eyes on us and denies us entree to the upper floors where he hoards his treasures. Chamonal Pere, chubby and bright-eyed, gesticulates, jabbers, and adjusts his two pairs of glasses as he sells us a Fournier, *Manuel Typographique*.

Clavreuil Pere, genial paterfamilias, is, as ever, just going to or returning from the hunt.

The personnel of their *librairies* has undergone a metamorphosis since our early visits in those days when "busy priests & satisfied nuns" walked the cobbled lanes of the Left Bank and drowsy cats and sleepy dogs basked in the sun. And so the journals that capture those years have become a period piece. Even as we made our annual visits we noticed the changes taking place. In England we were there, observing, when Irving Davis determined "to go in for more & more expensive & obvious books," and when our good friend Winifred Myers abandoned books to specialize in manuscripts and autographs. The taste of the times as well as the bent of the dealer and the availability of material determined and still determines those transformations. Today much of the book trade seems bent upon becoming purveyors of modern books written in English and protected with jackets in mint condition — books that demand few skills other than the ability to pay for them.

Some of the firms we visited early on have survived — Quaritch and Maggs, Thomas-Scheler, Clavreuil, and Chamonal. But more have succumbed. Here they are remembered — our greats, our eccentrics, our bread-and-butter suppliers. Here they take their places in a tapestry now complete and still vibrant with color.

The range of dealers in those days was surpassed only by the range of early printed books available for purchase. In England we could "walk knee-deep in books & climb a tottering ladder that sways among . . . piles & piles of books." In Paris "we learned early on that some of our most prized acquisitions" came "from the tiny warrens in the rear of French bookshops where treasures were hoarded until the 'moment juste.'" Books that had been placed in safe keeping for the duration of the war had by 1947 and 1948 been returned to the bookshops; privately owned libraries were auctioned or offered for en bloc purchase; even dealers who had lost thousands of books in the blitz or at the hands of the Nazis found themselves still in possession of books in the hundred thousands.

By the time we two voyaged abroad most of those books had been placed or replaced upon shelves and were for sale. At what other time in recent history could we two have been offered the run of "a wonderful library" that had belonged to the Marquis of Bute and was now in the hands of a dealer in Marylebone High Street, London, who "had scarcely grazed its surface." At what other time would we have been offered *sammelbands* of German Reformation pamphlets or 16th-century papal bulls, or 17th-century French political pro-nunciamenti accompanied by a dozen or more refutations? What other recent decade would yield us so many bound-withs — those unexpected works bound with the first item in a volume and often far surpassing it in interest. The Old World might have been low on food and minus many of the comforts of life, but during the decade of 1947 to 1957 early printed books were available en masse.

Their availability was such that, scanning our purchase ledgers for the decade, we can select almost at random one noteworthy acquisition after another. During our very first book-buying trip abroad in 1947, in a cluttered shop on London's Cecil Court, we found a Luther Sermon of 1519 whose title-page was adorned with a woodcut medallion portrait that was the earliest known likeness of the great Reformer. The sermon was accompanied by a small col-lection of Reformation tracts, each of which pro-rated to the cost price of $11.25.

The year 1949 also yielded treasures. From Allen on Grape Street we carried off the Beaumont landmark on the Gastric Juice printed in Plattsburgh in 1833, a work that revolutionized gastro-enterology. Its price was $19. At Irving Davis' we found that "glori-ous fete book" of 1550 by Grapheus, a folio celebrating the visit of the future Philip II of Spain to Antwerp, complete with all its plates, and the copy of a distinguished 17th-century French historian. Its price: $72. The same fruitful year we acquired from the firm of Bernard Quaritch for $360 the *Philosophical Transactions* of the Royal Society in a run extending from 1665 to 1702, filled with sem-inal scientific papers by Boyle and Newton, Ray and Leeuwenhoek.

The 1950s continued the promise of the late 40s. From a small dealer on Paris' Left Bank, Leconte, we purchased in 1952 for $42.80 the first French edition of Descartes' *Principes de la Philosophie* in a superb copy bound in vellum. The next year brought us, among many *alia*, that great find of the Fernandes de Queiros, the pamphlet on the Terre Australe issued in 1617 that is one of the milestones in travel and exploration. For that gem, bought from Picard on the rue Bonaparte, we paid 37¢. The first edition of Henri Estienne's account of the Frankfurt Book Fair published in 1574 was more expensive. It cost us $56 when we acquired it from that genial scholar Ernest Weil of Golders Green in 1954. Then, in 1955, from the cornucopia of Hilde Rosenthal's establishment in Hilversum, we carried off the collected writings of the eminent Italian humanist Pico della Mirandola published in Strasbourg in 1504, in a copy bearing an ownership inscription of 1505. Pico cost us $27. The same year we found on Francis Norman's shelves in Hampstead the first book to emerge from Robert Boyle's library — an attack on the Jesuits priced at $4.04.

Such books as these are highlights indeed, but their stature is equaled by a great many other purchases recorded in our ledgers or mentioned in our journals for the years 1947 to 1957. Such books were there — in London or in Paris, in the Netherlands or in Italy; they needed only to be recognized for what they were and snatched. Of the few we have singled out here to memorialize, prices ranged from 37¢ to $360. Today such prices are meaningless. It must be remembered that prices are always relative and dependent upon supply and demand; it must be remembered that one could live in London during that period for about $30 a week per person. And it must be remembered that we in turn sold those books for a profit that might range from smallish to double the cost. Today, four decades later, the prices of most of those great books would be astrophysical, and — more to the point — many of them could not be found on the open market.

We ourselves are in great measure responsible for such a state of affairs. It was we, and dealers like us, who sold so many of our finds, our greats, our landmark books, to the nation's developing libraries. Librarians, having found the purchase of books extremely difficult during the war years, now were making up for lost time and filling empty shelves with the hallmarks of civilization. And, unless deaccessioning was sanctioned, there they stayed — our Pico della Mirandolas, our Descartes, our Beaumonts. Just as we had formed happy relationships with the foreign dealers who supplied us, we shaped strong friendships with the librarians to whom we sold: "Molly" Pitcher of the Folger, Donald Wing of Yale, Mabel Erler of the Newberry, Felix Reichmann of Cornell, John Fall of the New York Public Library. All are gone now, but the books they accessioned are, for the most part, still very much alive.

Between the buying and the selling of antiquarian books, as we have often emphasized, is the phase that demands most of the dealer and brings him/her the strongest gratification. This phase is devoted to the study of the book purchased. All dealers and collectors naturally gravitate to a particular type of book. Their background and education, their tastes and interests lead them into one field or another: science or art, history or literature, law or medicine; plays or novels, poems or technical treatises. We two have always been fascinated by the Sherlockian arts of historical or literary detection.

L. in her office

Indeed, one chapter of our first collaboration, *Old & Rare*, is entitled "Holmes & Watson." Hence we are lured by the innocuous looking bit of ephemera, the volume with an intriguing title, an anonymous or pseudonymous work — books that require study so that they can be adequately described and offered to potential customers. In this phase of bookselling, Holmes and Watson feel most at home.

And so we sought on foreign bookshelves those "Italian or French inconnus which we can work over," those "small Italian Renaissance works that we love." We took pleasure too in viewing one book from many angles, seeing different facets in a single volume. In a work on the Garden of Eden we could find not only serpents and apples but — for a geology customer — mountains. In Campo's great folio on the city of Cremona we could find — for a collector of Judaica — the signature of a Jewish engraver on a map. In a manuscript travel diary written in 1820 we could perceive a Shelley source.

Collections of political ephemera would soon present special opportunity for research and discovery. When in the course of our Bibliographical Decameron we found in 1947 at Nijhoff's in The Hague a small collection of 17th-century French political pamphlets, an interest in historical ephemera was awakened in us that would intensify into a passion. A few years later, at one end of the rue Bonaparte in Paris, we found at Roux Devillas a larger collection of those short tracts that encapsulated so much history — those "unbound pamphlets that carried on-the-spot reports of battles and coronations, births and deaths, assassinations and reforms, alliances and hostilities." As we added to our trove of such ephemera, studied their contents, digested their messages, we sensed in such throwaways an immediacy and a timelessness missing from more grandiose tomes. Stimulated by our undergraduate and graduate studies at home, we relished unlocking such keys to political history. When we found collections of those 16th- and 17th-century on-the-spot reports and commentaries abroad, we found them irresistible.

And so our own training and the foreign bookshops we were exposed to had, so to speak, interweaving influences upon us as well as upon the nature of our business. Whenever it was possible we dealt in those books and pamphlets where we could find a detail or a comment, an image or a reference that had been overlooked by other researchers. The minutia we unearthed helped open up the past.

Another European visit — to the Erasmushaus or Haus der Bücher in Basle led Holmes and Watson to write a novel they called a "Biblio-Folly." Entitled *Quest Book — Guest Book*, this is the saga of the search for a most extraordinary copy of Erasmus' *Praise of Folly*. The search ends, as so many do, both happily and unhappily, and we conclude our *Quest Book* with the statement that "What really mattered was that [our copy of the *Praise of Folly* had survived almost 5 centuries and . . . was a testament . . . to humankind itself, and the enduring human mind. . . . We were its baggage masters so to speak."

Are not most antiquarian dealers the baggage masters of the books they buy and study and sell? Surely it has been as temporary custodians of books that we two have lived out our 20th-century Bibliographical Decameron. That Decameron marked several other bookish occasions in addition to the purchase of rare books. It was punctuated by two memorable International Congresses, one in occupied Vienna in 1954, one in liberated London in 1956. It encompassed also an event of significance in our own lives — our tenth anniversary in the rare book business.

Now we have passed our fiftieth anniversary, and one of our editor-advisers has asked us to answer the query: "What did you do between your trips abroad?" By now the answer must be obvious. We did what every other bookseller does — we studied, we catalogued, and we sold the books we had selected abroad. However, Rostenberg and Stern did a bit more than that. Both Holmes and Watson have always lived double lives — the life of the bookseller, and the life of the writer. Between 1947 and 1957 those double lives were active indeed. During that fertile period, Rostenberg wrote and published in *The Papers of the Bibliographical Society of America* and in *The*

Library full-length articles on the lives and careers of seven 17th-century English printer-publisher-stationers. She had researched their activities not only in American libraries but in London at Stationers' Hall and Somerset House. Eventually those articles on "John Martyn, 'Printer to the Royal Society,'" "Richard and Anne Baldwin, Whig Patriot Publishers," "Robert Scott, Restoration Stationer and Importer," "Nathaniel Thompson, Catholic Printer and Publisher of the Restoration," "Robert Stephens, Messenger of the Press" "John Bellamy: 'Pilgrim' publisher of London," "Nathaniel Butter and Nicholas Bourne, First 'Masters of the Staple'" — would join others as chapters of her compendium on 17th-century English printing and publishing.

Stern too would take time between book-buying trips abroad to add to the roster of printed books. Her writings during the Bibliographical Decameron included her biography *Louisa May Alcott*, published in 1950; her *Purple Passage: The Life of Mrs. Frank Leslie*, 1953, a biography of a colorful 19th-century American woman publisher who was also a femme fatale; her exercise in imaginary libraries entitled *Sherlock Holmes: Rare Book Collector*; and her collected volume on 19th-century American publishers entitled *Imprints on History: Book Publishers and American Frontiers*.

Between 1947 and 1957, as during every other decade of our lives and partnership, we have been combining the writing of books with the buying and selling of books. This is an antiphony in which we are still engaged. Our journeys abroad in search of books have enriched both aspects of our lives. After 1957 we continued those journeys, but we no longer kept journals. There were no more letters dispatched home from Paris or London, Amsterdam or Vienna. With the deaths of our parents, we had lost our audience.

Now our earliest ventures abroad in search of books are made available for what we hope will be a more extended, if not a more enthusiastic, audience. Here will be found adventures that may amuse, anecdotes that may enlighten. Here will be found a forgotten world born out of war, struggling for peace, a world of rigidity and austerity and want, but a world alive with books. The vellum-

and calf-backs of centuries past still gleam on its shelves; its book-sellers still flaunt their erratic eccentricities; and these two explorers still traverse the highways of London, the cobbled lanes of Paris, the colorful purlieus of Europe in search of the Old and the Rare.

1947

―――――――――――――――

THE NEW YORK TIMES, JULY 29, 1947

SAILING TODAY

Transatlantic

VEENDAM (Holland-America). Rotterdam Aug.8: sails midnight from 5th St., Hoboken

LR JOURNAL » **August 2, 1947**

Frankly, I don't know how to keep a diary anymore & don't know why I am except for the fact that in the months & years to come such impressions are of interest to read, revive years & memories. . . . Now [aboard S.S. *Veendam*, Cabin 475] as if in my dreams but actually in reality we are going to Europe to buy books!

RETROSPECT* Although these opening lines were indeed prophetic, they did not reflect the mixed emotions of two bibliophilic Magellans. The snapshot taken by a shipboard acquaintance shows us on the verge

Bound for the hunt on the Veendam, *1947*

of a great adventure as we posed on the upper deck of the *Veendam*. However it does not reveal the inner trepidations of these two jaunty voyagers. As we well knew, Europe still suffered immeasurably in 1947 from the war and its aftermath. Very few American dealers were venturing abroad. Our parents' concern about our plans heightened our own anxieties. And once aboard the S.S.*Veendam*, we realized this would be no luxury cruise. Mady, who had taken a deluxe voyage abroad with her mother in pre-war days, noted the contrasts:

MS JOURNAL

. . . There are many changes discernible: the type of passenger, for one — no teachers, no tourists. . . . In our small cabin on D deck way below water level, there are 3 instead of 2 — the 3rd in our case being a refugee from Nuremberg, Mrs. Valerie Kunreuther, whose life includes a governess in her ancestral home; the Nazi terror; a voyage on the *Navimar*; and now housekeeping and catering in New York — and visiting the daughter in England whom she has not seen in 8 years.

---

*All Retrospects are by both LR and MS.

LR JOURNAL » **August 9**

We are in London which fact is becoming more realistic as I look out upon Marble Arch & hear the rather strange inflection of the voices around us. . . . The *Veendam* docked yesterday at Southampton ca. 2:30 & we reached the harbor ca. 4:30. The customs were very simple & I suppose we both regretted our lack of cunning & failure to have brought in more cigarettes. The customs house at Southampton was merely a temporary shed, the original one having been bombed. From the very moment the train pulled out for London we saw the vestiges of war-smashed buildings, shells standing as mute evidence, twisted iron work, windowless buildings. . . . At Waterloo we grabbed our luggage & arrived at the Cumberland. . . . London is perturbed. . . . At breakfast we had to stop eating as the waiters launched a surprise strike which forced us to dine later at the elegant Grosvenor House . . . tail-coats & nothing to eat — cube bouillon, spaghetti most tasteless & a caramel custard plus chicory coffee amounting to $2 each. Well the waiters at the Cumberland returned & we dined in its grill room where we have reserved a table for the entire stay. Tonite we had good lamb, vegetables, potatoes, a roll without butter & a dreadful "sweet" — coffee & tea not included & no napkins are served either here or at the Mayfair Grosvenor. One is not permitted to spend more than 5 shillings plus the house charge & the extras such as coffee or tea.

Well, as to the purpose of our trip — we visited Thorp's in Berkeley Street this a.m. He has an excellent stock of books but he is quite steep. We picked out 10 of which I think we'll get 7, but will return for another glance. The bulbous-domed Mr. Harris was very affable. One of our purchases includes a beautiful copy of the great work by Domenico Fontana on the erection of the Egyptian Obelisk in the center of St. Peter's Square, replete with engraved plates of the feat — printed in 1590 — $12.

RETROSPECT The $12 price tag for the first edition of Fontana's magnificent work on the Obelisk will — like most prices mentioned in our journals — prove incomprehensible to present-day readers. Everything is relative — more or less. In addition, it should be remembered that,

Thorp's, Berkeley Street, London,
August 1947

although food was in low supply, books were plentiful. Many dealers had retrieved their stocks from the country where they had kept them during the war. Now they were eager to sell. However, there were not many eager Magellans floating around London's book quarters. A large supply plus a small market equaled a fine opportunity. It is true that Thorp's copy of the Fontana had a facsimile half-title — but all the plates were present in splendid impressions. The next year in Europe we would buy another copy for $56 and in 1949 a third copy for $44. We sold the Thorp copy to an architect, Edmund Prentis, for $85, and priced the other two copies at $100 each. Since then we have not had a copy of the Fontana in stock. Probably today it would fetch at least $2500.

MS JOURNAL & LETTERS » August 9 & 11

In between bookhunting there is London — a dilapidated, bomb-stricken city where the forms flourish still without the substance. . . . We have seen many a bombed-out building in our walk along Park Lane, where so many buildings are charred, full of holes or just shells. It is *still* appalling.

LR JOURNAL

This a.m. & afternoon we had magnificent book hunting. We visited McLeish who had some very nice items — particularly 16th century — & was an affable, voluble book dealer. Later at Grafton's we found tremendously good stuff & would have been happier if the ladders had been higher & Mrs. Grafton not quite so snappy & worried about the invoice — also if she had removed her hat once & not sat shrouded in a corner eyeing us cautiously. Mr. "Elzevier"

Copinger was a most disagreeable gentleman who failed to smile but Mr. Peddie greeted us as the author of Strasbourg printing & informed us that he was the former St. Bride librarian, unfortunately now an employee of Stinkweed Grafton. But we bought lots & all good. I must say that the settlement of the £22 14s invoice occupied the time & hands of Messrs. Peddie, Copinger, Madam Grafton & the shipping clerk, while we skidowed about confusing them all by the additional purchase of a splendid De Thou binding.

In the afternoon we visited an elegant pseudo-Oxonian refugee, Bondy, who had some nice stuff. In short we have purchased 51 books in 2 days & at this rate by Saturday we'll be finished & won't have to worry whether the first course is the roll or the tea.

L. at McLeish, London, 1947

RETROSPECT "Some very nice items" at McLeish indeed. One of them was the first edition of Geiler von Keysersberg's *Nauicula penitentis* or *Ship of Penitence*, published in Augsburg in 1511. Its title woodcut depicted the ship with a preacher at the helm and was the work of the celebrated German artist Hans Burgkmair. This important work in the cycle of the Ship of Fools was priced $21. Other "nice" McLeish offerings included an illustrated 1550 *Decameron* and a 1508 German legal imprint that we passed on to the Harvard Law Library.

As for the Grafton establishment and its denizens, we have written about them in *Old & Rare* where we explain that Mrs. Grafton was not Mrs. anything but Fanny Hamel, a fairly popular author. Copinger and Peddie were both distinguished bibliographical scholars cowed by their employer. From the termagant Hamel we purchased the life of another termagant — Catherine de Medici — written by the printer-scholar Henri Estienne II and published in 1575. That was priced at $3 and sold to the Newberry for $15. For $8.40 we acquired Jacques Auguste de Thou's copy of a Hierocles bound in calf with the owner's arms gilt-impressed on both covers, which we transferred eventually to the shelves of Harvard. To our Grafton trophies we also added one of the rarest of Renaissance plays — the *Tre Tiranni* of Agostino Ricchi published in 1533 and performed in celebration of Charles V.

LR JOURNAL » **August 13**

It would be advisable to carry this diary about in order to record the sensation of visiting Messrs. Maggs, Goldschmidt & Quaritch. We actually entered 50 Berkeley Square which breathes elegance and elegant books. Maggs is a champagne dealer.

Quaritch has not only great books but always something of interest, particularly when we can afford to buy. Picked up some nice Aldines.

We then proceeded to Davis & Orioli where we were greeted as "Miss Leonie Rostenberg." The books were superb but the prices terrific. We have some in consideration.

In the afternoon dropped in at Allen where we picked up the Estienne New Testament in the Grecs du Roi, a magnificent copy. This 1550 version will be perfect for our 1950 catalogue.

E.P. Goldschmidt

The highlight of the day was a visit to Mr. E. P. Goldschmidt of 45 Old Bond. He was really most genial and courteous to two very poor little book dealers. He showed us some of his great rarities: his Münzer, Froben's copy of Tortellius, some of his Gothic bindings, & was much like a modern Grolier or Dibdin, thrilling his guests in his snug room. My entrance was not quite comme il faut, having missed aim &

fallen to the floor in the presence of his elegant & precise assistant Randall. The purchase of books from Mr. G. was quite a problem — his prices of course are exorbitant. Ray's *Travels* $55; an unimportant humanistic treatise $37.50. Finally, to relieve the tension and make his poor bewildered visitors happy, E.P. let a copy of Murmellius, *Versificatio*, go for $11.25. But it was a happy & exciting visit.

RETROSPECT Would it be possible today to visit such a quartet of dealers in a 24-hour span? Quaritch and Maggs survive, it is true, but antiquarian dealers of such stature are few and far between. Davis and Goldschmidt are no more, alas. Their tremendous knowledge and the scope of their stocks enriched us in our beginning. We learned from both, and we expanded our holdings from their bookshelves. They were our mentors and our friends.

As a matter of fact, many years later, in 1986, Madeleine did an article for *AB Bookman's Weekly* entitled "Reminiscences of Book Buying in England — 1947" in which she mentioned the momentous purchase of the Murmellius for $11.25. That reference called forth the following communication from E. P. Goldschmidt's successor Jacques Vellekoop:

"Your article in this week's *AB Bookman's Weekly* brought back many memories. At first I thought that it was quite impossible that you could have bought a 16th-century book for $11 — as your first purchase from E.P.G. But yes — here it is. You might be amused to have a copy of the original 'slip.' As you can see it had appeared in two catalogues before: First in Catalogue 49 no. 179; and then in List 30 no. 250. The stockbook number 19485 tells me that it was bought on 19 November 1937 as part of a sammelband from "Hess" and that it cost 5 shillings, plus the cost of binding, which was probably 2/6.

The entire slip was of course in E.P.'s handwriting, except for the Annotation 'Rostenberg, 12 Aug 47' which was in Randall's handwriting. And the book was located on K3, which was the bookcase on the left of the fire-place, on the third shelf.

How things have changed!! I am writing this on my computer terminal, which will print this out on several kinds of paper, by pushing button F11. I worked out that £2.15.0 (or rather £2.75 nowadays) is $11 — as the £ was $4 then — on my solar-powered calculator. Our computer also tells me that your last purchases here in September 1984 included a Moxon, 1677 for $4000 . . . twice your whole 1947 budget."

On that same halcyon day in August 1947 when we added Goldschmidt's Murmellius to our stock, we bought from Irving Davis for $12 a collection of humanistic treatises by Pico della Mirandola published by Froben in 1518 which we subsequently sold to our friend Felix Reichmann at Cornell. For the extremely rare edition of Vasari's Life of Michelangelo with the woodcut portrait of the artist and a view of Florence on the title-page, issued separately from the collected Lives in 1568, we paid Mr. Davis $20. One of the "nice Aldines" we picked up from Ted Dring at Quaritch that morning was Isabella Sforza's philosophical treatise of 1544 on the tranquillity of the soul. Another was the life of Cleopatra by Giulio Landi, the first life of the Egyptian Queen in the vernacular, published in 1551 by the Aldine Press. Davis had priced it at $9. Signora Sforza went to the Newberry Library where Stanley Pargellis received her with joy; Cleopatra journeyed to Yale where she was suitably welcomed by Donald Wing.

MS JOURNAL » **August 15**

The afternoon was wonderfully successful, for we bought 14 books from Breslauer on Museum Street. He is a most Anglicized refugee. He knew his stock & therefore sold us a lot, & it was a humanistic feast. L & he schmoosed on, very much at home in the Renaissance.

Books seem to be more plentiful than anything else in London. Food so scarce that, with three courses permissible, one is a roll. The natives get 1 ounce of lard & 2 of butter & 1 rasher of bacon a week. . . . No wonder the speakers in Hyde Park chide Wall Street and America — how can they face their problems after 8 years of chronic hunger & chronic fear. The nation is in a deplorable way & tho they have the grit to face war I do not know whether they can face this peace. "Work or Want" is the slogan — but how can they work on the diet they have & with their caste system that still makes them so preoccupied with unessential formalities. Tailcoats forever never mind the emptiness on the plates.

From Mrs. Black [a family friend] we got our closest approach to the Battle of Britain. Standing at what was once 138 Seymour Street, looking down over the wall that the city has erected over the rubbish & garbage of the emptiness, we heard her tell us where each room had been in the Georgian dwelling she had reconverted into doctors' offices. A bit of the black & white tile was left. Otherwise nothing. . . .

In the afternoon bought more from David Low on Cecil Court just off Charing Cross Road, where L raced another customer through a newly issued catalogue & for once we got what we wanted.

LR JOURNAL » **August 17**   *"Work or Want," Billboard, London, 1947*

It is impossible to record all we've done but it seems that we buy even more as I buy even in my sleep. But for once our book buying is not a dream but magnificent reality. And yesterday we really made our find. We bought a collected volume of 16 early Luther tracts which I believe are really something — the one bears a woodcut of M.L. & I don't think we're far from wrong in guessing these are tremendous rarities — also a collected volume of Estienne material — all of this found at a dealer, E. Seligman, 25 Cecil Court.

Friday we visited Ifan Fletcher at Wimbledon. He conducts his business as we do, in his home, & has a very comfortable place with a fine garden. He introduced his wife who was pleasant and unstylishly English, but we deeply appreciated her as she served coffee & cake. It was a warm, good visit & we got some very nice Italian books, also some University of Paris tracts which appear to be extremely interesting. As a matter of fact, the major portion of our purchases are 16th-century & I shouldn't be surprised that the 1949 catalogue will read "The Renaissance & Reformation."

RETROSPECT If ever there were a study in contrasts it would be the portraits of Ernst Seligman and Ifan Kyrle Fletcher. The former, a transported Teuton with a bad temper who held sway in a warren on Cecil Court that yielded not a single spot empty of books. The latter a smooth, well lubricated Welshman whose home in Wimbledon was his well organized castle devoted to his theatrical specialty. From both, however, we could purchase books — books that did indeed go toward building up our Catalogue No. 5: "Renaissance & Reformation." The catalogue appeared not in 1949 but in 1948, and one of its highlights, if not its greatest highlight, was the Luther *Sermon* with the earliest known likeness of the Reformer. It was a medallion portrait by an anonymous artist and it had, we deduced, been impressed from a medal struck in Luther's honor, since the profile and the lettering were in reverse. It showed Luther in his monk's habit and biretta, and it appeared within a circular roll intersected by a rose bearing a caption. Printed as it had been in 1519, the portrait preceded the likeness of Luther executed by the great German artist Cranach in 1520. Luther may have delivered his sermon to contest points of faith with his adversary, the Catholic Eck. As far as we were concerned, it had been delivered to carry his portrait across the ages to both of us.

The contrast between Seligman and Fletcher was apparent even in their stocks. Fletcher dealt mainly in theatrical materials, and from him we acquired that day a delightful peepshow.

LR JOURNAL » **August 19**

On the book front: visited Marks yesterday — it's a huge place & I'm certain they have more tucked away than we dug up, but one is slightly hesitant to poke too far to the left on the highest rung of the ladder, & we are now becoming choosy.

Today we traveled afar over a poorly paved road in a poorly springed bus to Tunbridge Wells where we saw Dobell, a tottering, feeble-voiced gent who was more eager to pack his valise than to sell us books. He has mostly English stuff but we found 5 — none too good but adequate — also another

Percy Dobell, Mt. Ephraim Road, Tunbridge Wells, 1947

item in a shop near the Pantiles — I'm not yet certain just what they are. The town is interesting, hilly, full of odd shops and smelly fish markets, & I felt very far away & happy in my profession.

August 22

Cambridge is in my mind — one of the great & glorious spots of England. I don't believe I have had a greater feast for the eye than the Gate of Edward III leading into Trinity College, walking through that beautiful expanse of quadrangle, watching the sun play on the carved figures of Edward & the Black Prince (I believe) & walking through to the green river Cam cutting through the sward & guarded by the drooping willows. . . . It was a rare, full aesthetic experience & a "first" of the stay. I thought the entire town lovelier than Oxford — more undisturbed & architecturally more beautiful. All of this visit was enhanced by the purchase of splendid books at Bowes & Bowes including a contemporary Cambridge binding by Nicolas Spierinck — a beauty. We got little at Heffers to my surprise.

Our friends the Snewings dined us Wednesday at the Cafe Royal exuberant in red plush & a gay spot of Wildeian England. I found it none too *Wilde* (ha ha) but it was a very comfortable & pleasant evening.

RETROSPECT As appropriate as the Cambridge binding was our Bowes and Bowes purchase of the 1568 Caius-Kaye debate on the comparative antiquity of Cambridge and Oxford — a chauvinistic debate still carried on.

Bowes & Bowes, Trinity Street, Cambridge, 1947

MS JOURNAL » **August 21**

Yesterday we bussed to London Bridge, passing the worst devastation in London — along Cheapside — whole blocks torn out — but the view from London Bridge over the Thames with its bustling tugs, toward Tower Bridge, was marvelously like old times. We framed in our mind's eye the age of Henry VIII comfortable on a royal barge with trumpets fanfaring & heads falling.

LR JOURNAL

In the afternoon we visited a suburban dealer near Golders Green, Ernst Weil, who was much older than I had imagined, & most agreeable. He is still very German in his manner & seems to live in a similar state — here about 14 years. He was the head of a former large Munich firm and is most reputable & well-known. We bought 9 wonderful items from him, 16th-century. Have bought 85 16th-century books — my favorite period. We have indeed bought well — also bought a Franciscan Flemish MS which appears to be interesting.

LR JOURNAL » **August 25**

This trip has . . . taught me the lesson of war — it just doesn't tear you apart physically — *then* you're done for — but emotionally when you have to go on — that's the hard part. But at a tea party at Mrs. Black's yesterday, Lady Slipper-Snapper regarded "war as sport" & "the poor Germans must be fed — they simply cannot starve, my deah." Incredible. The company consisted mostly of hyphenated names, correct posture, powdered sandwiches, & the ingredients of Mrs. Black's birthday cake. The English still love their lords & ladies, despair of the commoner, the labor-wallower, can't understand ice-water, dislike Americans or find them entertainingly odd, do agree that you can't beat the Jews at finance. They are clever & have long noses which look down at their tasteless meals with warmth & approval.

MS JOURNAL

It's wonderful how the English revered Roosevelt. The genteelly traditional, the leftists of course, the plain middle class — all reverence him as a great man & a great American. He would have helped them in their present plight & they know that. They distrust America now, but still look to us for help — as they helped us when we played for time in the war. The English still muddle along until they face the last ditch — & then (I hope still) knuckle down to business. Just now they're certainly muddling — stopping business for tea, more fond of leisure than work, & their sleeves however frayed make a fine flourish. We saw this sign in a Tunbridge Wells tea shop:

DON'T GROUSE!
When you miss your "Roasts & Gravies"
Give thanks for the Royal and Merchant Navies.

They don't grouse much, I must say, & face the decline of the British Empire with finesse if not with fortitude. If they do go out of the picture they'll go out with a perfect bow & most graceful "alarums & excursions." I doubt if "nationalization" on a socialistic pattern is the deepest desire of the majority, but perhaps it may be. Luxuries here: a pineapple $6; a nectarine 30 cents. A purchase tax of 100% on clothing. The people eat horse & whale meat instead of beef.

This has been a great experience for us — certainly not altogether joyful but most interesting, & we have some idea now of what war can do to a country that is supposedly victorious.

LR LETTER » **August 27**

This a.m. we had to drop in at the Holland-America Line to find out about sailing home — it was a madhouse: people waiting to get back & no reservation for 3 months or more. Of course all Europe wants to get to America!

LR JOURNAL

Went out to Farringdon Street Market where the "barrow vendors" begin commerce at half after ten. Found a copy of Varchi & 2 early 18th-century tracts. We can be very pleased with the books — they are really beauties & we're thrilled about them — bought an additional

L. at Farringdon Street Market, August 1947

8 at Davis & Orioli. . . . Mr. D. reminded me of a literary hobgoblin.

MS JOURNAL

Heinrich Eisemann, who looks like an aging Satan, invited us to inspect his stock. He lives in an apartment — Clive Court — in Maida Vale, & the flat was crammed with books — most of them beyond our means but we did get 2. He has mostly German, Spanish & Italian works particularly 16th & 17th centuries — so it was quite a treat. We are learning also how to accommodate buyers in a shop. For God's sake let them have a big table, a chair and an ash tray — & if they want to browse, let them.

Our stay here is nearly over. Though certainly not unadulterated pleasure, it has been most enlightening.

MS JOURNAL » **August 31**

To begin at the beginning: on August 28 we left London on the Golden Arrow — a very deluxe train that took us to Dover, where we boarded the *Invicta* & sailed thru a choppy, bracing Channel to Calais. There we entrained on the Flèche d'Or — very fancy waiters flying down the aisle every minute with a different course, many

Brunier's, 1947

of which were "suppléments" not included in the price of the meal — melon, meat . . . We got to Paris at 5:30 p.m. & drove to the Lutetia. . . . We walked in the evening, finding the streets of Paris very quiet — most shops closed for the "congé annuel" — needless to say, everything terribly expensive — a peach 50 fr. — a complete dinner about $8. Breakfast the next morning consisted of the leadlike bread & hot water, to which we added our own G. Washington coffee & our own sugar. The hotel's breakfast, consisting of ersatz tea or ersatz coffee, & a confiture from Africa, was, as the maître d'hotel remarked, "pas fameux." With this beginning, we raced to the bookstalls, which do not open till 10:30 — & found only modern books. However, at Brunier's, across from the stalls, we did get 3 charming 18th-century books.

. . . Most of the life in Paris seems so underhand — it is the city of the black market — that is its solution of post-war difficulties, whereas London's is austerity, grimness.

LR JOURNAL » **August 31**

We took a 12:30 train for Strasbourg. . . . I can't imagine how I ever stood Strasbourg for 3 and 1/2 months — it is so provincial, poor & limited. Unfortunately gabled houses and dormer windows don't fascinate me any longer & the miserable sanitation exuding a mixture of cabbage & excrement disgusted us. Also the books proved vastly disappointing & Argentoratum of old had little to offer of its great humanistic past. It appears that the Germans plundered the shops & left a few Hachette editions & copies of *Alsace Illustrée*.

RETROSPECT LR had researched her doctoral dissertation on early 16th-century publishing in Strasbourg during the summer and autumn of 1936. Those pre-war days when the Nazi threat was beginning to take shape have been described in her chapter "Strasbourg am Rhein" in *Old & Rare*.

MS JOURNAL » *Strasbourg*

Leona's librarian friend from 1936 — François (Franz) Ritter — invited us to lunch and we immediately showed him our Luther find from Seligman. When he saw the 1519 vignette of Luther he immediately said, "C'est inconnu!" — a great discovery. The 16 tracts for which we paid $180 are worth over $1000. They may be worth even more, as we believe the tract containing the vignette (cost $11.25) will fetch at least $250.

The stained glass has been removed from Strasbourg Cathedral, & the thing is a symbol, for the stained glass & color have all been effaced from weary, post-war, poor, poor Europe. We are weary, after only one month, of a Europe minus stained glass. It is not old Europe & never will be again.

LR JOURNAL » **September 7**

Our stay in Switzerland [2 weeks repose in Interlaken] answers the prayers of these two D.P.'s. The gemütlichkeit of this Swiss holiday brings balm to the soul.

LR JOURNAL » **September**

At Basle we rushed forth to Haus der Bücher where we were greeted by a deep obeisant bow from Herr Doktor Seebass. . . . He showed us some beauties of the Renaissance which we bought, among them 2 splendid Erasmus items, the Froben first of the *Encomium Matrimonii* & a handsome Badius edition of the *Praise of Folly*. What books! and to add to our keen joy we bought them at the very spot which housed the Decor Hollandiae — the Stupor Mundi — Erasmus Roterodami. Here he lived from 1534 to 1535, having been the guest of Jerome Froben. This is the original "Haus zum lufft" owned by Jerome. I was disappointed that they had not left E's chambers intact, but forward geschäft even in Basle. The stock room below still has the original timbered ceiling, black with age, as in the days of Jerome Froben. It was quite an experience.

RETROSPECT The appropriateness of buying books by Erasmus in the very house where he lived for a time made a deep impression upon us. We were to use the experience in a collaboration published in 1993 entitled *Quest Book — Guest Book: A Biblio-Folly*. The book we quested was of course a *Praise of Folly*.

LR JOURNAL » **September 17**

At The Hague we bought splendid books from Nijhoff — really grand — including 15 belonging to the *Soldat François* cycle, all bound in one.

And so we head for America with our mission accomplished, having purchased 280 books of which 250 are superior.

RETROSPECT The *Soldat François* cycle consisted of lively political pamphlets written in France between 1604 and 1610, some urging war, some urging peace, some probably penned by a former cook named Maitre Guillaume, many anonymous or pseudonymous. Like all good

Martinus Nijhoff, The Hague, September 18, 1947

ephemera, they restored the past graphically. We were to assemble many large collections of those tracts in the future and would devote an entire catalogue, *One Hundred Years of France 1547-1652*, to describing 755 of them. Our early encounter with such printed throwaways at Nijhoff's on the Lange Voorhout in The Hague kindled in us a passion for French political pamphlets that still abides.

The New York Times, Sept. 29, 1947

Incoming Passenger and Mail Ships
(*As Reported by Wireless)

Today

From	Will Dock
VEENDAM, Holl.-Amer. . . . .Rotterdam, Sept. 19 . . . .3 P.M., 5th St, Hoboken	

1948

THE NEW YORK TIMES, AUGUST 13, 1948

SAILING TODAY

Transatlantic

NIEUW AMSTERDAM (Holland-America). Rotterdam Aug.21: sails 4 p.m. from 5th St., Hoboken

MS LETTER » **August 22**

. . . Only a complete idiot could be in a sightseeing mood in present-day London & we are not yet complete idiots. Life is really too drab here to give a damn about Catherine Parr's old woodwork.

We just came in from a stroll down Park Lane which is still all battered & damaged — all those beautiful elegant houses.

The food situation has not improved perceptibly . . . but they do have grapefruit this year, and the roll is not a course.

LR JOURNAL

. . . Visited Grafton Sat. a.m. where that old hex Miss Hamel . . . still guards her wares in flounces of black satin, a broad-brimmed hat & a large piercing brooch. . . . Old Peddie was schlobbering about, dilating upon his Index — now containing 250,000 entries & in the 4th Supplement. Anyway we purchased 23 good books, the majority being Italian & French Renaissance.

Monday morning we went to Davis & made a bigger haul than we ever did before or ever dreamed of doing. He had just returned from Italy, & therefore was well stocked with the small Italian Renaissance works that we love. Since he means to go in for more & more expensive & obvious books, it is well that we bought while the buying was good. Other dealers seem to feel as Davis does, & soon there may be no more opportunity of getting our type of thing in any quantity at all. Among the items we got is a collection of 95 Italian legal & economic tracts ($20 for all) which we shall break up, bind, & we hope sell to Harvard. . . . Many interesting things & some beauties. In the afternoon Davis drove us to his warehouse in South Kensington, where we culled 16 more nice items from a cellar of miscellaneous stuff. . . . Also Davis promises to quote us this sort of work & so we may get more from him if the books pass through his hands.

Hofer (of Harvard) was at Davis's when we got there. He praised our scholarship, loved the way we did things, said it was first rate, & told us to be sure to go to Harvard. He was most complimentary!

On Tuesday morning we went to McLeish, where last year's brother was on hand — just as "affable" as his relative. We bought 11 Renaissance items & had tea & cake at 10:30 a.m. in the room overlooking Little Russell Street. All very charming. McLeish discoursed more on politics than on books — thought there was a strong pro-Russian though not pro-Communist feeling here — and bowed down to Roosevelt which pleased us very much.

RETROSPECT 1948 seems to have been no improvement over 1947. London was as heartbreaking as it had been the year before, still battered, still woebegone, still lacking decent food, still suffering from its Pyrrhic victory. Actually we were tempted to turn on our heels and run back home if a return voyage had been possible. The presence of war vestiges in all their horror still revolted us and exacerbated our customary hypochondria. A contemporary English reader will certainly comment: "Horrid, spoiled American brats!" And they would be right. Somehow the glory of the great city filtered down to us through the ruins and lifted our hearts. Fortunately, we resisted the impulse to retreat because London was as rich, if not richer, in books than it had been in 1947.

It is ironic that, of all the books we bought at Grafton's from "that old hex Miss Hamel," one went back to England to the firm of E. P. Goldschmidt. That was an early English comedy entitled *Pedantivs* by Edward Forset, performed in Cambridge in 1581 but not published till fifty years later. It provided its original audience much amusement at the expense of English educational institutions, and it provided us with finely engraved portraits of the scholar characters who in our view much resembled Messrs. Peddie and Copinger of the House of Grafton.

And, speaking of education, that "big haul" we made from our friend Irving Davis included the first edition first issue of John Locke's *Treatise Concerning Education*. His book could have been written today instead of in 1693, criticizing as it does the current curriculum — as we continue to do in 1996. In a different field was the set of Vasari's *Lives of the Artists* that we bought from Mr. Davis — the first illustrated edition of 1568 with woodcut portraits of all the great artists including Leonardo, Raphael, Titian, and of course the incomparable Michelangelo. In his turn Michelangelo had immortalized one of the early feminists — Vittoria Colonna — whose sonnets we plucked that same day from Davis' shelves and would sell later on to our prime feminist collector Miriam Holden, about whom more anon.

As for that "collection of Italian legal & economic tracts ($20 for all)," we did indeed disbind them and sent them on their individual ways to a variety of institutions including the nearby London School of Economics. Of course many did go to Harvard. It was a wonderful coincidence for us that we met Philip Hofer at Davis' that day, because Philip Hofer was then the curator of Printing and Graphic Arts at the library of that most prestigious institution where we planned to dispose of some of those tracts. Thereafter, every time we visited William Jackson at the Houghton Library, we took time to drop in on Mr. Hofer, sometimes to offer him a handsome illustrated book, sometimes just for a chat. As a result of all this, Mr. Hofer one day — quite unwittingly — almost became a member of the firm of Leona Rostenberg Rare Books.

The senior member of our firm was always disinclined to use the wastepaper basket. She habitually saved scraps of our stationery on which a few notes had already been typed or mistyped. After our return from abroad, she used one of those discarded sheets of 8 1/2 by 11 business paper to order from our printer another 1000 sheets of firm stationery. "Please print up exactly the same heading, etc.," she instructed him carefully. The printer followed her instructions as carefully. When we received the 1000 sheets they read as follows:

LEONA ROSTENBERG RARE BOOKS

152 East 179 Street
New York 53, N.Y.

Philip Hofer, Curator   Madeleine B. Stern, Associate
Dept. of Printing and Graphic Arts

We never told Philip Hofer this story. We were quite certain he had never entertained the idea of departing Cambridge for the Bronx. Nor could we lay the blame on our printer. We must, we decided, confiscate the sheets without divulging their existence to a living soul. In the end — and very characteristically — we simply cut off the headings and used the remainder as scrap paper for more notes to be saved by LR.

LR JOURNAL » **August 25**

In the afternoon to Feisenberger, who used to work for Davis. He had some very nice stuff & we added to our stock very happily. F. is a red-headed refugee with an establishment on Duke St., mincing ways, but nice, very nice books.

RETROSPECT One of the books we bought from "Feisy" provided us with a distinguished new customer — the New Orleans attorney and collector Edward Alexander Parsons. The copy of Giraldi's *Hecatommithi* that we acquired from "Feisy" for $14 had provided the Bard of Avon with sources for *Othello, Measure for Measure, Much Ado,* and *Twelfth Night.* It provided us with our introduction to the Bibliotheca Parsoniana. We would continue to supply that library with appropriate items from time to time, including several Aldine pocket editions of the classics. A decade later, in 1958, the Bibliotheca Parsoniana would be acquired by the University of Texas, and moved in three sealed vans containing 750 cartons from 5 Rosa Park, New Orleans, to Austin. Then, in 1962, Edward Alexander Parsons died.

Not long after, when booksellers were still discussing the transfer of the Bibliotheca Parsoniana, Rostenberg and Stern paid a visit to New Orleans. The founding member of the firm was especially interested in tracing her family residences, for her mother had been born in the Crescent City, and her partner Stern was equally interested in tracing the residences of Mrs. Frank Leslie, the New Orleans belle turned New York publisher, whose biography she had written. Needless to say, both partners were also interested in visiting bookshops.

One of these was a combination antiques and antiquarian book establishment. It offered a hodgepodge of porcelain and china, tumbledown chairs and nondescript jewelry. In a dark little area we spied a bookcase, and immediately gravitated to it. On the top shelf perched five or six small morocco- or calf-bound volumes that we immediately examined. One was a classical text in a charming Aldine edition in pocket format that had once no doubt been secured in the saddlebags of some Venetian traveler. As we opened now to the first flyleaf, we noted that it had traveled far indeed, for there we saw with considerable amazement the pencilled collation marks of LR and MS. This was one of the pocket Aldines we had sold to Mr. Parsons, and it should have been tucked into one of those 750 cartons that had transported the Bibliotheca Parsoniana to Texas. Instead it sat upon the bookshelf of a New Orleans antiques dealer. Edward Alexander Parsons had written shortly before his death a book entitled *The wonder and the glory: confessions of a southern bibliophile.* Now, in *Old Books in the Old World,* we two confess that we were too timid to investigate the presence of a book with our collation marks that we had sold to Mr. Parsons and that still sat on a New Orleans bookshelf. Perhaps it had dropped out of a carton on the journey from New Orleans to Austin. Perhaps it had been detained by a pilferer.

A few nights later, over dinner with a New Orleans colleague, we told the story of the book that had somehow found its way to the antiques dealer's establishment. His reply was terse: "That guy should be buried in cement at the bottom of the Mississippi."

This little biblio-mystery has never been resolved. But every time we see a pocket Aldine classic we think of it. Indeed, we think of it whenever we recall our 1948 visit to the red-headed Mr. Feisenberger with "mincing ways" and "nice, very nice books."

LR JOURNAL » **August 26**

Thursday the 26th took the suburban train to Wimbledon where we again met "that charming Welshman" I. K. Fletcher. The Fletchers accepted our gifts, which included a Manhattan Telephone Book lugged 3000 miles brought at their request. We bought 12 books from him, mostly Italian Renaissance like the majority of our purchases this year. He returned to London with us (after 11 a.m. cake & coffee) & regaled us with tales of his theatrical interests. It seems Laurence Olivier is a customer of his & models his acting in part on the books & prints he buys. He also told us of a find of Mexican imprints he once made.

August 27

The high cost of low living is the general summation of la vie Anglaise. We watched the English queuing up to buy their fish & meat, with ration books, in long lines. Requests everywhere to provide your own wrapping paper, otherwise you get some old newspaper or nothing to wrap your purchases in.

We bought 3 tomatoes & ordered bread & butter & tea back at the hotel, & had tomato & our cheese from home as sandwiches for lunch. Very good & we'll do it again.

People are much less friendly than last year — things are so bad with them — bus conductors, waiters, all very surly. There's a little rebuilding going on, but nothing much to speak of. We bought a lit-

tle guidebook to London & every other place is marked with an asterisk indicating it has not yet been reopened because of war damage.

We saw "Cage Me a Peacock" at the Strand Theatre. The the-
atres here run from 7 to 9:30 p.m. — a leftover from war days. In
between we had tea, bread & butter & crackers — served in our seats
during intermission.

When things go off ration points it seems they also go off the
market.

At dinner the other night we ordered custard, but were told we
could spend only 1s 8d (35 cents) more & the custards came to 2s (40
cents) — so we had to have 1 custard and share it.

The movies don't start till 4:30 on Sundays. The cheapest seats
are also the best — that is, the closest to the screen.

LR JOURNAL » **September 1**

We are awaiting breakfast in our room as we do almost daily. This
first meal, somewhat troublesome to confront, usually consists of
mushy, sour plums, dry-as-dust cereal capped by thin dirty milk, a
greyish roll & mealy toast. . . . Lunch is usually a home-cooked meal
of tomatoes purchased from a street barrow, sterilized, soaked, rinsed
& peeled by the firm, & thickly sliced, alighting on bread ordered
from dear old Room Service. This is our best meal — the dinner is
usually a ghastly procedure served by nasty brown-uniformed girls
who resent all Americans. The food is completely unpalatable.

Little of London of the past remains. The shops are ugly, the new
stores unattractive, the streets smashed & the people largely apa-
thetic.

This a.m. we visited one dealer. He didn't have too much but I
do think we found a rarity unknown to Mr. Wheeler of Harding, a
grubby Holborn gentleman who rose from the ranks. He represents
Hollywood's idea of a commercial gent, with a rolling moustache,
red nose & stunted height. At any rate, we found the posthumous
edition (the first) of Spinoza's greatest work — & I only hope it is
complete.

RETROSPECT It was. The only work published under Spinoza's own supervision, the *Tractatus Theologico-Politicus* was issued in 1670 with a fictitious Hamburg imprint. Actually printed in Amsterdam, it was of course placed on the Index. Bound with the copy we found at Harding's was a 1674 refutation of the work. Even in 1948 it was underpriced by Mr. Wheeler at $11. But it was still underpriced when we sold it to the Newberry Library for $65.

September 2

Yesterday was quite a day — rich, full, varied. In the morning we had the bookbuyer's dream fulfilled. Went to Francis Edwards on Marylebone High Street & were most cordially received by Mr. Harris, who showed us upstairs & downstairs & all over. They had a marvelous stock & what is more, Mr. Harris very kindly lopped off prices until we were able to carry off 14 lovely items at very agreeable prices. It was a full & rich experience. The bated breath with which one glances at the shelves — the expectancy of taking down a vellum- or English calfback, the thrill of opening to a Renaissance title-page with a charming woodcut or floral border — these are so inherent a part of the booktrade & such a pleasant concomitant of it that it is really a pity to buy just from catalogues.

During our peregrinations we passed an odd little paper shop owned by one Kettle. In we popped, as we saw some attractive binding paper in the window. Well, we bought 6 dozen sheets — simply charming — the same papers cost at home ca. 40-50 cents per sheet — here we bought them at 14 cents a sheet. . . . It was the oddest, quaintest shop — we just adored it.

Loaded with a heavy tube, we taxied to 45 Old Bond, the stronghold of E. P. Goldschmidt. I suppose a visit to E.P. is much in the same category as a novice prostrating before a patron saint or a pet high priest. It is the stamp of the man & the history of his firm. There is no difficulty in selecting books. Here humanism exudes from the shelves. . . . To visit G. is a definite experience, & since he is the last of the truly great bookmen we are very fortunate to have been permitted this experience a second time.

The evening was one of decided contrast. We visited friends of the family — the Prykes — on Seymour Street, and the visit, I must say, rendered us almost insensible after this glorious day of genuine books. Joy held forth on the nobility of slops at the Duchess of Kent, the agility of the Princess Alexandra at making beds, and the coronet worn by the Duchess of Anglesey. The English are all 18th century in their adoration of court life & gossip of Elizabeth's noble virtues — a flawless damsel who was abandoned on the dance floor by Philip, who, mind you, won't rat like Edward Eight, etc., etc.

RETROSPECT One of the books we purchased from Francis Edwards' establishment on Marylebone High was an atypical one for us, but we could not resist it. It was the work of an English engraver John Carwitham, and consisted of twenty-four copperplates of all kinds of floor decorations. Each plate had a top portion designed to give ladies the entertainment of coloring it! These two ladies refrained from following Carwitham's suggestion and instead sold him to the New York Public Library.

As for E.P. Goldschmidt, who has been enthroned in our *Old & Rare*, we continued to find elusive humanistic texts on his shelves at Old Bond Street — treatises on the demise of a little-known queen or the welcome extended to a visiting monarch — ephemeral writings, individually of no great stature, that nonetheless restored so much of the life of the European continent during the early sixteenth century. E.P. knew the significance of such trifling works, and we learned much of that significance from him.

There was probably as much history to be learned from the attitude and comments of our family friends, the Prykes of Seymour Street. Gossiping about the royals, they were certainly in love with the pageantry of the past — a pageantry glorified far more in our early books than in the London we witnessed in 1948.

September 4

This morning we visited Francis Norman on Gower Street. He is a man who could a tale unfold. He lost his wife, child, and books in the blitz. . . . Norman sells only to a few American professors & universities, but he did sell us 6 books, one of which he threw in gratis in case any should be incomplete.

RETROSPECT This was our first visit to the gentle, uncertain Francis Norman whom the blitz had estranged from life. We would visit him annually for many years. Neither he nor his surroundings ever really changed. He would marry again, and move from Gower Street to Hampstead Heath; he would have other children. But nothing about him ever really changed. He remained an alien in his own land always. One year — as we shall recount — we found a great sleeper on his shelves. We often thought that inside Francis Norman there must be many turbulent nightmares sleeping on, not quite ready to explode. His strange ghost appears and reappears during our first decade of bookbuying abroad.

LR JOURNAL » **September 5**

We took a 9:45 train for Oxford, arriving ca. 11:30. We first visited Rosenthal, a member (younger one) of the great German house. We were greeted there by his associate, a huge walrus-looking individual with a dark beard, sonorous voice, and unceasing affability — Dr. Maurice Ettinghausen, to whom I had written reams when I worked for Reichner. At first he didn't understand my name and said, "Oh, the cousin of Leona Rostenberg of New York." I said no — it's Leona herself. He said he knew all about me. We were introduced to their dog, who was named just like mine — Bonnie — after Bonaventure Elzevier!

Later ploughed up to Blackwell where we were greeted most warmly by Mr. Lincoln. He has a prodigious memory. Congratulated M. on her articles, her camera and herself — & let us pick about. He carried books to us, gave us the proofs of a new catalogue & joked & chatted — results: 13 books with the possibility of another 3, much pleasure & strengthened business ties. He then directed us to Fullers where we tea-ed & just made the London train.

LR JOURNAL

Visited one Baer, a refugee, whose family, originally from Frankfurt, was among the greatest of all dealers. It was really very sad as his stock was completely liquidated by the Nazis. He had so little & was so eager to sell. As a matter of fact, I had visited his brother

Leo in Paris in 1936, & our meeting here established a pleasant entente cordiale. He lives in a shabby apartment & it really hurt.

RETROSPECT At the time I could not help contrasting this visit with the one I had paid to Mr. Baer's brother Leo in 1936 when I was a neophyte in books. Then Leo Baer displayed to me in a luxurious Parisian setting his equally luxurious books — a Grolier binding, a Pompadour binding, Books of Hours, early woodcut books. There was nothing remotely resembling any of this at the modest home of his brother exiled by the war to Cricklewood.

LR JOURNAL

This a.m. we tried Thorp. He is so very expensive. . . . Harris remarked that he believes his books have reached the maximum — I hope so. We bought very cautiously but I was very glad to get another copy of Isabella Sforza & also of Vittoria Colonna — nice Renaissance items. Also got a 1523 Aeneas Sylvius with a fine Cologne border which may be a Woensam at first glance.

September 12

Thursday a.m. we browsed about on Shaftesbury Avenue & picked up an excellent work at Allen's — Allwoerden's Servetus. In the afternoon we green-lined to Guildford. . . . Enjoy tremendously traveling through the countryside & arriving at a bookish destination, finding a town on a hill, the spire spoking above the distant green, & the smell of the fish markets pervading the streets, the windows filled with cheap fruit tartlets alive with wasps, & the long, usually wrong walk toward the bookshop which in this instance was Traylen. It is quite a fine shop, large, spacious & attractive. Mr. T. was away but his assistant Mr. Lane, who knew nothing about books & wore

L. at Traylen's, Guildford,
September 1948

his tie pulled through a heavy ring, proved very gracious. We bought a few nice items & the fine Ackermann print of the Bodleian Library.

. . . Friday we visited the Sackville West estate — the great Elizabethan manor house at Knole. We ate our sandwiches near the entrance to the great park. It was exceedingly beautiful, quiet with drooping oaks of tremendous age, green silvery lights, opaque mists, mosses climbing the stumps, & everywhere fawns & deer gamboling about, bringing to reality the life of Tudor England. The manor was far more embattled & crenelated than I had imagined, consisting of towers & courts, 52 staircases, 365 rooms, 12 exits & entrances, 7 something or other, etc., etc. The interior thrilled me less, despite all the majolica, Stuart furniture, Tudor pewter, and my last duchess on the wall.

RETROSPECT The Allwoerden we acquired at Allen's on Grape Street was a singularly important book on two grounds. This study of Michael Servetus, early 16th-century Spanish theologian, explored the subject's life both as freethinker and as scientist. Servetus was burned at the stake for his views, and Servetus also investigated the nature of the circulation of the blood long before Harvey.

Instead of being burned at the stake, Mary of Scots was beheaded by order of her cousin Elizabeth I. One of the "few nice items" we bought from Traylen was Adam Blackwood's defense of Mary. Blackwood, the Scottish Catholic, had visited the queen during her captivity in England, and after her death published a volume that exposed her treatment in prison and denounced Elizabeth for the death of an innocent.

Just recently we were graphically reminded of our visit to Knole, when we attended a performance of *Vita & Virginia* performed by Vanessa Redgrave and Eileen Atkins. The magic of the Sackville Wests persists.

LR JOURNAL » **September**

In the a.m. a most cordial visit to Joseph. He is one of us & really put himself out greatly, taking us all over, cutting prices, & discussing his friend Winston Churchill. We acquired a copy of the Holbein *Dance of Death* for $6 — a later edition.

September 14

The pièce de résistance was our visit to Peter Murray Hill, the combined dealer & actor. He is better looking than in the films & ever so charming. We acted like real New York fans, & remembering one of his roles, I greeted him vociferously, "Oh, you're the nice one!" We found some very attractive books, tea-ed with him & schmoosed. It was simply delightful. His wife is the lovely Phyllis Calvert. M & I really were excited.

This a.m. we achieved the ambition of childhood & saw the King & Queen en route to the opening of Parliament. We joined the general crush at Whitehall to behold the remnants of English pageantry — the colorful horseguards magnificent in scarlet, burnished steel helmets, plumes, jackboots & their lambskin saddles, the household cavalry & the Irish State Coach bearing HRM George VI & Elizabeth Regina. The people were not too demonstrative in their acclaim, but all waved, including LR Bibliopola Novi Eboracensis. . . .

In the p.m. we visited Myers & to my surprise bought 6 nice books — not too expensive. Now I am too weary & too full of England, bookish, heraldic and otherwise, to arrive at dramatic conclusions.

RETROSPECT The books we bought from the past-president of the ABA, Winifred Myers, in 1948 included two other accounts of Mary Stuart, a biographical compendium on the rulers of Venice, and a discourse against Savonarola — all 16th-century imprints. Winnie Myers would shortly abandon books for autographs, and though in the future we would not buy books from her, we would become fast friends.

MS JOURNAL » September 7

In the afternoon bussed out to Weil. . . . Mrs. Weil summed up the English very well, I thought, when she described them as a free nation with very rigid conventions. I want to record some of the things I've learned about England in 1948. What is it doing, this free but rigidly conventional nation?

1. Meat — 1s 2d per week per person, of which 1 shilling may be spent on carcass meat & 2 pence on corned meat. I took a picture of the butcher shop in Seymour Place, where a sign was hung in the window regretting that no OFFAL was for sale. I passed another butcher shop with whale steaks in the window. Tonight at dinner I heard an Englishman loudly ask the waiter, "Is it horse or beef? I heard the Cumberland served horse."

2. Health — The National Insurance for Health is in pretty full swing. Every person pays £12 a year & gets full service: doctor, hospital, etc. The doctors get a few shillings per head per year, but are enrolled with some 3,000 patients. A wonderful idea when it works out.

3. Radio — much better than ours — no commercials & very highbrow programs — good music. Only 3 stations, however, to choose from: Light, Home Service, & the Third (highbrow), with Overseas as a possible fourth.

4. Press — rank! — no news — no newsprint to speak of. "Woman Found Dead" frequently in a flat. "General Dies of Poisoned Fish." Auto crash. Ads.

5. People — filled with tradition, convention, understatement. Imitating America in a crude sort of way. Lacking the breadth & freedom & scope of American people.

6. The city — a provincial place compared with New York. Iron holders for the 18th-century linkboys to use for tapers still stand in front of bombed-out Georgian houses — a symbol — like the stained glass gone from Strasbourg Cathedral.

RETROSPECT We never were served horse meat at the Cumberland, but we were certainly served whale. It resembled beef all right, in its roseate color, but to make sure we asked the waiter who replied matter-of-factly, "Whale." We omitted the meat course.

Suffering from an imaginary disposition from the uneaten whale and all the other food we should have eaten but did not, Leona consulted a medical friend in London. He arrived at the hotel laden with two large bottles of medication in pill and liquid form — enough to supply an army with pharmaceuticals. "I don't want all this stuff, David."

"But it's free, love," the doctor replied. That evening Leona, frugal as ever, offered all her medicinal bounty to the chambermaid. Her reply was an eloquent commentary on National Health Insurance: "Oh, lovey, I don't need it — we get it all free — throw it out!"

Another time, after a bout of imaginitis appendicitis, we both consulted the hotel doctor whose advice epitomized the hazards and discomforts of postwar England: "Everything's filled with sawdust," he informed us. "Go to Switzerland where you can get fresh eggs, or go back home."

MS JOURNAL

In the afternoon we tried our hands at London shopping. Everything *sounds* so simple when you read that all you need is A) a Tourist Voucher obtained by cashing $100 or B) a passport & order to send your purchases to the boat or America. We went to the Board of Trade in King William Street near the bank to ask about our books & were told all would be OK & also that other purchases would be free of purchase tax. When we got to Harrod's, however, we found another story. In the first place, only a few articles — for export only — are free of purchase tax — a little linen, some china, a few handbags — nothing personal. In the second place, even when you buy for export only, you get entangled with red tape. L was fortunate enough to find a charming china tea set for her mother, but in order to buy it she had to go down to the Export Bureau of Harrod's, produce passport, change money, & pay 17s 6d for crating & sending to the boat. Harrod's is a large store with its own bank, restaurant, etc.

Umbrellas, worth about $5, cost $15 because the purchase tax can't be removed. Blouses worth $10 cost $25 for the same reason. The only things worth your money are antiques — if you can find them. The salesman at Harrod's told us he wakes up at 5:30, gets to work at 7:30, and 3 times a week doesn't get home till 9 p.m. Wish we could feel they're all working that hard. Personal shoppers would be a godsend for tourists but they don't have the men.

I for one am eager to return to book buying. I like it better than sightseeing. Low just left his catalogue & L is poring over it looking for advance bargains. Let's hope!

September 9

More Londinopolis items come to mind — e.g.:

1. Petrol — they are getting enough to go 50 miles a month. Cars sell for thousands of pounds, even ancient models.

2. Dogs — so wonderful the way the English treat them. They cuddle up on owners' laps in buses & the conductor comes along to pet them — no leash, no muzzle. I think every English person loves a dog. Treat them as they do children, who are given extra rations & really look in the pink.

Hied to Buckingham Palace for the Changing of the Guard — very drab now in contrast to the full regalia of pre-war years. The Changing is the same, however — the marching, stamping, presenting arms, saluting — England won't relinquish its traditions, though they're clothed in army drab & khaki now. The band played, of all things, Strauss waltzes! In some ways England is too civilized.
. . .

The New York Times, Sept. 21, 1948

Incoming Passenger and Mail Ships
(*As Reported by Wireless)

Today

	From	Will Dock
NIEUW AMSTERDAM, Holl.-Amer.	. . .Rotterdam, Sept. 14	. . .3:30 P.M., 5th St. Hoboken

1949

THE NEW YORK TIMES, JULY 22, 1949

Outgoing Passenger and Mail Ships

Today

NIEUW AMSTERDAM (Holland-America). Rotterdam.

LR JOURNAL » July 30

. . . The boat (*Nieuw Amsterdam*) was enhanced by a galaxy of miscellaneous celebrities:

1. Dr. Albert Schweitzer who resembled a Fuller mop. He ate exclusively with his knife & carefully cut 9 olives as hors d'oeuvres.

2. Three Bourbon princesses & prince. Le prince s'est assis avant ses soeurs qui prièrent toujours avant les déjeuners & toutes les repas. It was etwas. He was the Prince de Bourbon without throne but with good appetite.

3. Violinists: Nathan Milstein & Isaac Stern.

4. The Channel-to-be-Champion, one Miss France, who has been copiously photographed by the *Evening Star* & who stuck her beaming head out of the coach at Waterloo.

5. Erich von Stroheim, former villainous movie hero who resembled a small H. Goering.

LR LETTER

. . . We passed through the British Immigration authorities & the one who looked at my passport & at me said, "Oh, I recognize you from last year!" & M's inspector wanted to sell her a book he had. So you see business looms up!

We took a short bus ride — a bit of repair seems to be going on, but it still shocks one to see completely guttered streets, shambles & weeds rampant in the heart of London.

MS JOURNAL » July 31

Yesterday a.m. we began our book hunting, spending the whole day at Davis'. He was a little more normal & a little less "elfin" this time — most amiable — & will take us to his warehouse on Thursday afternoon. We bought 42 books from him, spending $505, & ordered 4 more from his forthcoming catalogue. Among them are some magnificently illustrated books — the 1550 *Triumphe Anvers*, which he had priced higher last year, but which we now got for $72. It will look beautiful opened up in a downtown window. Also the Dutch entrée of William III in Holland (we have the English at home) & the Stück-Schiessen, a charmingly illustrated folio on archery. We're well pleased, as most of the books will make good solid stock — contents solid & interesting — & enhanced by 3 or 4 elaborate works. It was fun, but also very exhausting, but we were glad not to have to waste the Saturday before Bank Holiday. Everyone else at Brighton, munching on a sardine.

RETROSPECT By now we had grown more familiar with that pipe-chomping Italianate Englishman Irving Davis. His enchantment with the books he had selected in Italy was contagious, and when we looked at them we envisioned them adorning the show windows of a downtown office we had so often considered. We never got the office but we did get the books.

Where would we find today two such glorious fête books as the Grapheus *Triumphe d'Anvers* of 1550, issued to celebrate the visit of the future Philip II of Spain to Antwerp the year before. The handsome folio was enriched with 29 plates by the Flemish artist Coecke and remains one of the most splendid Renaissance entrée books. The copy we bought from Davis had been owned by the distinguished 17th-century French historian Etienne Baluze. The same day we bought from Davis another fête book honoring a later royal visit. The text, by Bidloo, the monarch's physician, described the return of William III of England to his native Holland in 1691. That folio boasted 15 plates by the great 17th-century Dutch engraver Romein de Hooghe.

Our interest in women's history antedated the general impulse in that direction, and so we acquired from Irving Davis a study published in 1607 of the life and death of Lady Jane Grey by Michelangelo Florio, closely associated with Shakespeare's circle. He too, as preacher to the Italian Protestant congregation in London, could be described as an Italianate Englishman. As feminists we were even happier to find on Davis' shelves a vellum-bound copy of the rare 1562 edition of the collected writings of the illustrious Renaissance scholar Olympia Fulvia Morata.

Standing on a ladder viewing Davis' new stock, we opened a slim Latin book dated 1594, bound in boards, and found ourselves comparing its horrors to the more recent horrors of Nazi Germany and World War II. The anonymous *Dolium Diogenis*, concerned with the wars against the infidel and the Turkish depredations in Poland and Hungary, was a *Dolium* not only of 1594 but of 1944. Eventually we would list this item in an entire catalogue devoted to the Turkish menace.

Davis interrupted our cogitations about the infidel to show us a handsome Baroque volume that we mention in our journal simply as *Stück-Schiessen*. This was a work by one Imhoff about a shooting match in Nuremberg in 1671, brilliantly illustrated with 5 double-page plates. What an item for those evanescent show windows! Instead, it went to collector Philip Hofer of Harvard in October 1949.

We recall with nostalgia that wonderful visit to Davis in 1949. His cat Ginger remained seated in a hatbox most of the time, but he himself hopped about almost frantically, so eager was he to share with us his enthusiasm and euphoria.

MS JOURNAL » July 31

In addition to our literary efforts, we unpacked the food compartment & dined last night on a bowl of vegetable soup heated on the Sterno. Everything done in great secrecy, as we stealthily set up the outfit & trembled when a maid knocked on the door. We feel like 18th-century smugglers, with locked doors, sentry posted & the little Sterno jollily cooking away. With crackers, figs & chocolate & a later tea & wafer snack we rounded out the first full day. . . .

MS JOURNAL » August 4

. . . To the aesthetic Mr. Breslauer, who regaled us with the story of how he lost his memory during a fall at Dieppe, & from whom we extricated 4 books. His prices are very steep & he has a keen sense of the rarity of Mr. Breslauer.

RETROSPECT Bernard Breslauer, destined to become an extremely distinguished antiquarian dealer and scholar, was at the time a brash and arrogant young man. He was the son of the well-loved Martin Breslauer of Germany. Bernard had all the marks of the displaced refugee, constantly stressing his superior knowledge. It is true that his shop on Museum Street boasted many fine humanistic texts that tempted us from year to year, but soon it became apparent that he set his bibliopolic sights far beyond us, preferring the titled upper classes as his customers in lieu of two Bronx commoners. The break was mutually acceptable, although years later, after his immigration to our country, the break was cemented especially when we had books that interested him.

MS JOURNAL » **August 4**

In the afternoon Davis drove us to his warehouse in his ramshackle little car, & again we explored the dust & debris of the cellar, finding 30 very lovely books moderately priced — mostly 16th-century. He's been so decent & sweet to us & he really has the sort of book we want: Italian or French *inconnus* which we can work over.

RETROSPECT One of those *inconnus* was a fascinating example of counterfeit printing. Executed in the 19th century, it purported to be a 1581 Aldine, and the copy we found at Davis' was bound in red morocco with the gilt Aldine Anchor on the cover. Its text was as interesting as its printing history, for it celebrated the prowess of the Scotsman, "the Admirable Crichton," who in 1579 visited Venice where he met Aldus Manutius the Younger. We have never found another copy of this particular *inconnu* that we bought from Irving Davis in 1949 for $12.

A genuine Italian 1581 imprint was also part of the Davis haul: Vieri's life of Petrarch's beloved Laura. It sat nicely on our feminist shelf until it was transferred to the Folger Shakespeare Library.

The search in Davis' warehouse yielded us a Shakespeare source: the *Historiae Brytanicae Defensio* of 1573 by John Price who introduced young William Shakespeare to the "Sir Hugh Evans" of *Merry Wives of Windsor*. Folger apparently already had that quarto, but the New York Public Library snapped it up.

Still rarer was the collected volume of 3 notable utopias published together in 1643 but today usually broken up. In one thick calf duodecimo we found Joseph Hall's *Mundus Alter et Idem*, Campanella's *City of the Sun*, and the *New Atlantis* of Francis Bacon who "took all knowledge for his province." That find — for which we paid $6 — was a bookseller's utopia for us. It went almost as soon as we returned, to our Alma Mater, Columbia University.

When L wrote in her diary shortly after our warehouse visit, she was obviously still bedazzled:

LR JOURNAL

To make this really a 20th-century Bibliographical Decameron I should be more steadfast & every evening sit down at this tea-stained cloth in Room 308 overlooking Hyde Park, Park Lane & Bayswater Road, & write of my impressions & the acquisition of books. We have bought a sound solid stock. . . . We have consistently avoided all Reformation tracts, particularly the dour physiognomies of Messrs. Melanchthon & Calvin; the commedie of Messrs. Cecchi, Giraldi & Firenzuola, and the poesie of Conti, Leopardi & gl'Ingannati.

. . . Oh world of books whose mountain we climb & view, hoping to find the great & unexpected — opening & closing — discarding or slyly keeping — "Hey Lee, this might be something" — "What do you think of this?" — "Na, put it back" — "This looks good — OOOOOH Yeh!"

LR & MS JOURNALS » **August 5**

The BBC Home Service is broadcasting an all-Beethoven program in the Henry Wood Promenade Concerts. We have just returned from one of the rare perfect days in bookland — a trip to Oxford. We spent the whole time there, where all is still the 13th century & it takes little imagination to recreate a pageant of the past.

We hied directly to Blackwell's where we were most enthusiastically received by our heavily pseudo-accented Mr. Lincoln who gave us carte-blanche to the entire store. Unfortunately they had no new exciting catalogue upon which we could pounce, but after ravaging the 3 floors we found 20 books, all of interest, including a fine copy of the 1550 Machiavelli — Joseph Smith's copy. Even if we don't go to Switzerland we are doing sufficient climbing in England, scaling the highest ladders & peaks of folios, viewing duodecimos & distant octavos with eager glance. It's such glorious fun — especially when you find something close to the ceiling.

RETROSPECT "OOOOOH Yeh!" The Machiavelli we singled out for mention was a large splendid copy of the first variant of the first edition known as the "Testina" for the head of Machiavelli that appears on the title-pages. The Joseph Smith from whose library it came was not the Mormon leader but the 18th-century British consul at Venice whose great collection formed the nucleus of the library of George III now in the British Library.

Other "OOOOOH Yehs!" included a 1521 Erasmus *Epistolae* with an Urs Graf title border and an 1850 Elizabeth Barrett Browning *Poems*, the second edition, but the one where *Sonnets from the Portuguese* first appeared.

LR & MS JOURNALS » **August 8**

The firm visited Maggs where we were personally escorted by Mr. Clifford himself. In this museum of monuments on Berkeley Square we were invited to inspect the lesser wares upstairs. We actually found 10 books we could buy, including a Hutten & a Spanish Life of St. Francis.

RETROSPECT We wrote much about "Mr. Clifford himself" — that sandy-haired, stammering young Englishman Clifford Maggs who seemed a bit amused that anyone would buy books under £200 — in our first collaboration, *Old & Rare*. After that book was published, *we* were both delighted and amused by Mr. Clifford's lengthy and exuberant critique in *Antiquarian Book Monthly Review* (May 1975). He exalted the book as "a model of arrangement and documentation, . . . written with enjoyment and wit, and with a fluency that belongs to born writers. There is a freshness in the impressions recorded that springs from the use of diaries and letters."

Mr. Clifford went on to describe his reactions to us: "I find the partners first visited Maggs in August 1949. . . . No words wasted, a quick greeting, and then to work combing the shelves, sometimes grumbling a little about the . . . prices! After two hours or so, I was summoned and the piles gathered together on our 'Pickwick Table,' the unpriced items priced (promptly accepted or rejected), and Miss Stern would sit down and record their purchases in a cashbook. When totalled up, she would ask if a cheque on account would suit us, and their visit was over.

. . . Strangely incurious about these two amusing ladies, I seldom spoke about them to colleagues, and confess that until reading their book retained the idea that Miss R was a refugee-bookseller from Germany, but I had been aware for some time that they were authors of scholarly bibliographical and biographical writings."

All of which illustrates graphically the intriguing problem of first impressions.

LR & MS JOURNALS » **August 8**

After dinner we took a long walk along the Bayswater Road to Brook Street & Clarendon Place. We are retracing the Forsyte family scene as we are re-reading *The Forsyte Saga*, catching glimpses of Forsyte 'Change thru the ruins, in realms where Timothy and the Aunts once lived, when London was the heart of empire. There are very few such glimpses left.

LR JOURNAL » **August 12**

Another perfect day at Cambridge where we made for the back of Trinity to picnic near the river. Why do the trees of Oxford & Cambridge swish with a particular rapture, why does the haze slightly cloud the sun, & why do the spires just pierce the blue? Because it's 700 years, ducky, of two great universities which can never be repeated on any spot on earth. Because it's 700 years of nominalism & realism, of Scotus & Aquinas, of English boys & English life — 700 years of great green quads & fountains & fuchsias & narrow streets & oriel windows & gabled houses & it's all the rich perfume & scent of these universities which fill our souls.

MS JOURNAL » **August 16**

Yesterday was another red-letter day in the third of the Trinity of our Book Hunts. In the a.m. to Quaritch where we met Mr. Dring, who assured us there was nothing in the stacks — only the one room of Continental material. We fooled him, however, for we bought what we had long ago set our hearts on — a 36-year run of the *Philosophical Transactions* of the Royal Society, Vols. 1 thru XXII — 276 numbers in all — 1665-1702 — the wonderful early ones with articles by Boyle & Wren & Newton, Ray & Leeuwenhoek & Willughby, & who knows what other shining 17th-century lights!!! It cost us £90 ($360) & we shall study them & sell them for a few thousand dollars. We were *so* thrilled. Even the redoubtable Mr. Dring was somewhat amazed, & reported to us confidentially that there *were* stacks & we might enter into their holy confines — which we did. In addition to the *Phil. Trans.* we bought a volume containing 11 early 17th-century French tracts right up our alley, & 8 other very saleable items. We taxied home, riding on air, & enjoying the thrill of the hunt — with the first 2 volumes of the *Phil. Trans.* tucked under our arms for research during our spare moments here & on the boat. We're very eager to mine the great treasure house in our hands.

RETROSPECT Mining that treasure house of the new science with its ground-breaking articles on blood transfusion, microscopy, theories of light and vision, innovations in chemistry and biology, proved productive not only for the firm, but for LR. It led to an important chapter in her book on 17th-century English printing history, the one on the printer to the Royal Society, John Martyn, and later on it led to her book on the Society's secretary, the avid collector and scientist Robert Hooke.

The wonderful day when we acquired the *Phil. Trans.* was climaxed by a visit to an exhibition that would have interested the 17th-century readers of that periodical extremely:

MS JOURNAL » **August 16**

In the evening we celebrated by attending the Colonial Exhibition at Marble Arch, where Londoners learn how "reluctantly their government took up responsibility for the welfare of Hong Kong & Fiji." There were fully dressed figures of Africans & Arabians — talking rooms — fish — tsetse flies — stamps — & what not, & we emerged from darkest Africa to board a bus for Richmond, where we continued our self-congratulations by ambling with the "commoners" along the Thames under a flaring cerise sunset. Henry VIII might be a bit taken aback by the cornet-eating, the suspenders, the "minerals" & fizzes if his barge came this way, but we found the sight of the boats along the river near the bridge, the great willows & the sunset sky still most beautiful. Back to the Cumb., where I opened *The Forsyte Saga* at an "Evening in Richmond" quite without design.

LR LETTER » **August 16**

We've had another wonderful day. . . . We had an appointment with Percy Muir, who is the head of the English Antiquarian

Booksellers Association, well-known throughout the bibliophilic world, author, dealer & gentleman. He met us in his ancient run-down little car at the town of Bishops Stortford which is an hour by train from London. Drove us to his home in the village of Takeley. His shop is attached to his house, which incidentally dates back to ca. 1580. It is an ancient timbered Elizabethan house, plastered inside and supported by heavy oak beams.

. . . After book browsing he announced: "Now we shall have lunch!!" You can imagine the firm's predicament. Being such fusspots, and worried about the possibility of English liverloaf, we had brought our own picnic lunch. We stammered & explained, but his wife Barbara, a masterful creature, shoved us into the dining room where a long board table had been set & the family assembled — 2 children & 2 cats. Well, we managed somehow: artichokes with margarine sauce, rice, onions, beans, tomatoes & bacon (they have pigs) stuffed with sausages & some odd jelly dessert topped with heavy English cream.

We talked of a hundred things, but of course mostly books, dealers, collections, customers, finds, etc. He had spent 8 weeks in Russia before the war, having been sent over by the English government to buy 3 great princely libraries & told us the most fantastic tales, all of which we lapped up. He told us of his visit to Prince Galitsin's library & of the Russian inability to come down to brass tacks or stick to any agreement at all. His talk was filled with tales of Belgian and Dutch dealers, French and Swiss, of books & their makers, & their buyers & their sellers. A day for the books!!!

RETROSPECT We found that day at Percy Muir's two publications bound together in red morocco and issued from the Aldine press of the Venetian Academy. Together they were priced $16. The first, dated 1558, was an oration by an Italian lawyer Natta on the word of God; the second, by a Venetian scholar Faventies, published in 1561, was on the origin of mountains. We decided to offer the two together to our librarian friend George W. White, head of the Geology Department at the University of Illinois. With him in mind, we also decided to forego any extensive mention of the word of God and concentrate instead upon the mountains. We resolved the problem by dilating in our offer upon the mountains seen from the Garden of Eden, and so we felt we had satisfied both the authors. We satisfied Prof. White, too, for he paid $40 for the combination. From that time on we realized that one book could be presented in many ways to different people — a concept that has frequently guided us in the study and sale of rare books.

Prof. White was sufficiently interested in our geological offers to include us in his rounds when he visited New York. He came for lunch one day, and sat between us at a table presided over by Leona's very charming mother. She was a marvelous hostess and, to make Prof. White feel at home, she introduced into the conversation anything of a geological nature that she could think of, mostly, as we recall, the geology not of the Garden of Eden but of an even more fertile subject for the purpose, the Grand Canyon. A few years later, after her death, Prof. White wrote to us, recalling his pleasure at the visit and especially the geological interests of my dear mamma.

MS JOURNAL & LETTER » August 17

Today was another marked in red, for we spent the entire day — morning & afternoon — at Francis Edwards in Marylebone High Street. We had already been there & bought 22 books, but Mr. Harris, our particular gent, was away at the time. Now he's back & reduced the prices of the 22 we had bought. He chinned with us, gave us the run of the place, and told us that a wonderful library belonging to the Marquis of Bute had just been turned over to him & he had scarcely grazed its surface. He told us to dig in & we had a marvelous time dipping thru all the calf and vellum books. We found 32 more — all extremely interesting & with his lopped-off prices more than reasonable. The Marquis of Bute's library, most of it uncollated, unchecked & uncatalogued, was the chance we'd been waiting for. We have never done better with our book hunts. We're the two busiest gals in London.

RETROSPECT Today, when we suffer from an austerity not of food but of books, how we dream of those "two busiest gals in London" sitting on the basement floor of Francis Edwards almost submerged by books of the 16th, the 17th, the 18th centuries. There were emblem books — the beautiful Lyonese *Pegma* by Cousteau with its 95 allegorical woodcuts in first edition of 1555, along with a later emblem book by Bocchi printed at his press in Bologna with 151 emblematic devices that had been retouched by Agostino Caracchi, the whole cased in a strap work binding from a 16th-century London atelier. Signor Bocchi sits today in the library of the Metropolitan Museum of Art where he arrived in April 1950 via Bologna, London and the Bronx.

We renewed our acquaintance with Robert Boyle, acquiring the Bute copy of the great chemist's *Experiments And Considerations Touching Colours* with the color chart, and — perhaps most exciting of all — we pounced upon a set of the specimens of exotic type issued by the Congregation for the Propaganda of the Faith between 1629 and 1776. This marvelous collection included alphabets and type specimens in Greek, Hebrew, Brahman, Arabic, Chaldaic, Georgic, Ethiopic, etc., etc. Today it is a triumph to acquire a single *one* of those exotic alphabets.

MS JOURNAL » **August 23**

. . . this afternoon . . . made us bless the rain that kept us from Brighton, for we found the Beaumont on Gastric Juice (Plattsburgh 1833) at Allen's on Grape Street. Mr. Berry showed us the slips for his next catalogue — & lo & behold! — there it was. Our hearts leaped for joy & we snapped it up for $19. Told him we wanted to give it to a physician friend so would take it with us, & it's reposing right on the table as I write.

RETROSPECT We have written in *Old & Rare* about this classic of physiology and our find of the rare first edition. We would add now that, several decades later, we found another copy of that pioneer experimental study for which we paid close to $1,000. That second copy of the Beaumont bore an autograph presentation inscription dated 21 Sept. 1852 from one M. B. Patterson of Decatur, Michigan, to a physician named B. P. Wells. Perhaps Mr. Patterson was showing gratitude to his doctor for the recovery of his health. Over 130 years later, M. B. Stern expressed her gratitude in the same way. In 1985 the firm presented to Dr. Henry Janowitz, the internationally known gastro-enterologist, that very same copy of Beaumont on the Gastric Juice. Once again history had repeated itself.

MS & LR JOURNALS » **August 26-27**

Goodbye, dear London. We leave your streets & red double-decker buses — your dark bookshops — your tea — your trade union-plus-royality enigma — your awful food — your thin, silly newspapers — your bewitching names, Tooting Micham, Wormwood Scrubs — your leftover gaslight — Goodbye, but we are taking you in our hearts.

Tomorrow we sail. How well we bought & how grateful we should be. London is most secure in our hearts & enduring. With all its difficulties, its austerities, so much will remain with us forever & become a part of a life which has been rich, loving & good!

1951

NIEUW AMSTERDAM (Holland-America) Southampton July 27, 1951. Sails 4 p.m. from 5th St., Hoboken. Letter mail for Netherlands.

LR & MS JOURNALS » July 29

And so the pattern repeats itself for the 4th time — a pattern that includes room inspection at the Cumberland, breakfast for 2 in Room Service, tea, tea, tea, red double-deckers, false fronts over bomb sites, and books. Wonderful books!

We do believe London is vastly improved in every respect.

Find again thrill after thrill in being back — thrills of the simplest nature — to see the parks, the people, the busses, all of London. The meal this evening was really good & all of London appears to

M. and L. aboard the Nieuw Amsterdam, *1951*

have improved considerably. We felt right at home — the clerks & waiters greeted us, & it was "cheerio" for 2 old book thieves. Dinner was a real improvement. Tomato juice (served by the wine waiter in a wine glass), roast beef, baked potatoes, string beans, roll & butter, and cheese (drawn up on a trolley — all varieties available now) & coffee. A complete meal — price $2.40 for both. One thing has gone up — the taxis — they're up 60%. . . . The pound has been devalued.

Started soon after our arrival on the book hunt. Saw Goldschmidt Friday aft. . . . still swaying with the *Nieuw Amsterdam* but bought 19 lovely humanistic books. . . . He's the same as ever, & gave us a noble audience. . . . Altogether it was quite a day, considering that we had breakfasted on board ship at 5:30 that morning.

Yesterday morning we visited Marks. . . . We received a hearty welcome & rummaged though 5 floors buying 12 books, one of which is a manuscript travel diary which was kept by an English traveler in Italy at the same time Shelley & Byron were in Pisa, and we feel it is excellent background material & can work it up. . . .

RETROSPECT That "manuscript travel diary" we found at Marks early on in the 1951 hunt was a notebook bound in vellum that had been purchased by a young English traveler in Pisa on 5 May 1820. In it, he proceeded to record his impressions and sketches of those very Italian villages where Shelley was writing his "Skylark" and his "Witch of Atlas." While Byron left Ravenna for Pisa, William Paget filled his notebook with pen-and-ink drawings that brought to life the current background of two great English romantic poets. We paid $11.20 for this treasure and after digesting its 95 manuscript pages, sold it for $75 to the collector par excellence who was specializing in Shelley and his Circle — Carl H. Pforzheimer. By serendipitous indirection, William Paget's notebook of a journey to Italy in 1820 had become a Shelley source.

MS LETTER » July 29

. . . In the afternoon went to Weil. . . . From him we bought 27 *entrancing* books — such a wealth of fascinating material over here. One contains the first color reproduction of an anatomical drawing — a gem. Another is a huge, gorgeous art volume with engravings of all the great paintings in Vienna in the 18th century. Also early botanical, medical & humanistic works — *marvelous* books. We have already bought 58 books, one fourth of what we expected to buy in the entire trip and have spent about one fourth of what we expected to spend. However, if we find such wonderful books as in the beginning, we shall buy beyond our allotment since we should, we think, gather our literary rosebuds while we are here.

. . . conditions are slightly better. They serve paper napkins — an innovation — & some of the bombed spots have been rebuilt or at least covered with false fronts, so the city does not look nearly so devastated as before.

MS JOURNAL » July 28

Yesterday we went to Francis Edwards both in the morning & afternoon — bought 22 books, all interesting — tho we had hoped for more.

Very varied selection: medical, geological, an interesting *Act* against unlicensed books, a short run of the *Phil. Trans.*, etc. Their stock is enormous, Mr. Harris very pleasant & ditto Mr. Love — tea was sent up to us while we climbed up & down the ladder, & down to the basement & up to the rare book sanctum.

In between the Edwards session, we sandwiched in not only the mid-day Sterno arrangement, but also the Sherlock Holmes Exhibit in Abbey House on Baker Street. Books, pictures, relics of the great man as well as a reproduction of his sitting room complete with chemicals, violin, letters, newspapers, pipes, cloak, hunting cap, etc., belonging to S.H. In the evening we took in a delightful movie — *The Lavender Hill Mob* with Alec Guinness — very English & much fun. At the New Gallery — 5th row — 2/4 (32 cents). . . .

RETROSPECT We cannot wait to retrospect about the books we carried off from Francis Edwards that red-letter day. One acquisition epitomized what happens sometimes to those who write books: an *Act* promulgated in England against seditious, scandalous and libelous works in 1649, five years after Milton's *Areopagitica*, his great defense of a free press. English political opinion during the 17th century was dramatized by two other purchases at Francis Edwards. We acquired an extremely rare mid-century tract entitled *The Bloody Court; or, The Fatall Tribunall*, a vehement castigation of Oliver Cromwell's bloody reign — printed throughout in red ink. At the same time we purchased a handsome folio volume illustrated by the Bohemian artist Wenceslaus Hollar and compiled by John Ogilby, describing the coronation of Charles II in 1661 at Westminster. Bound in calf, with the arms of Lord Stuart de Rothesay on both covers, it epitomized indeed a splendid occasion in English history — and an equally splendid occasion in our 1951 bookhunt.

MS JOURNAL » July 28, cont'd

And today we devoted to our familiar pilgrimage to Oxford — familiar but always fresh & always balm to the soul — the grey stone buildings so old, so old — the flaming geraniums on the green quads — the grey sky — lofty spires & turrets. We found a new & much loved spot when we wandered thru Queen's College & along a narrow walled passage. At its end was the Nuns' Garden — a quiet retreat of roses, where we sat together & thought the world well lost.

Another spot to add to memory. Incidentally, bought 3 books at Blackwell's including the *Letters of a Portuguese Nun* & an interesting pamphlet on the English Press at Oxford. Mr. Lincoln's A's as broad as ever tho his smile a little less so. A Mr. East in charge of rare books — cold as his name. After our picnic lunch (in our vacuum knapsack) at the Botanic Gardens, where we fed the birds as well as ourselves & sat before a pond of water lilies, we went to the Bodleian — old & new libraries. At the latter saw an exhibition of the 17th-century Bodleian — wonderful material devoted to the library & its librarians — Bodley — James — Hyde, etc. — & the donations, including presentation Bacons, Miltons, & other such. There we met Carl Pforzheimer, Jr., wife & children & L engaged them in lofty conversation. Another full & perfect day.

LR JOURNAL » **August 5**

Wednesday a.m. visited Davis where pandemonium reigned supreme & an antiquarian U.N. endured for a good 2 *hours*. Davis was his usual contained mysterious self, announcing a book or a price after a long suck at a dead pipe. He had with him Signor Cavallotti of Milan, to whom he introduced me as Signor Rostenberg. There was much scraping, bowing, shaking of heads & loud "si si's" — to which I replied, "Oh yes — oui oui." In the midst of these amenities his elegant secretary introduced the cat Ginger who showed little preference for a first of Ariosto or a first of Montaigne, & danced delicately across Caroso's handsome treatise on the dance with mincing feline steps. I was at this point on rung 12 of a ladder when . . . Lucien Goldschmidt entered. . . . D's books are still marvelous — the wonders, the very good, the good, & the few indifferent — all jumbled together — his prices however are extremely high & we only purchased 20 but we are returning.

RETROSPECT Of the 20, we single out the first French edition of Marat's great political pronunciamento, *Les Chaines de L'Esclavage*, which we sold to the University of Kansas; another plum — the earliest French treatise on the so-called monts de piete, the mounts of piety that were actually pawnbrokerages established by papal authority to lend money to the poor. Our discourse on those loan institutions was written by Signor Scarini and published in Douai in 1585. It went to Harvard. Still another purchase from Signor Davis carried both of us, but Leona especially, to a more immediate past. This was the *Heron Mechanicus* by Dasypodius, the great work on the Strasbourg Clock printed in Strasbourg in 1580. Leona, who had researched her doctoral dissertation in Strasbourg during her Columbia University days, never could have resisted this treatise on a time machine she had so often gazed at during her months alone in the Silver City. The *Heron Mechanicus* went soon after our return from abroad to Bern Dibner, collector of books in the history of science. From Davis' freshly opened crates, we had sent these birds of passage on to their final destination.

MS & LR JOURNALS » August

In the afternoon we bussed to Kensington to see Neville Armstrong of Peter Neville, M's English publisher. He gave us the jacket of her *Louisa May Alcott* & a 1951 list of his publications, including a page for *LMA*. Very English, very stammery, somewhat difficult, but quite pleasant . . . In the evening saw an excellent production of *The Three Sisters* which set a definite mood and was very effective — although we can't say it produced any desire for long draughts of vodka, heavy snow & dark evenings immersed in a shadowy drawing-room reading Chekhov & longing for MOSCOW.

RETROSPECT *Louisa May Alcott* is M.'s biography of Louisa May Alcott which had first been published in 1950 by the University of Oklahoma Press and was about to be reprinted in England. Today, 46 years later, the biography is once again being reprinted, this time by Random House, and this time as a consequence of all the recent Alcott excitement engendered in part by a new film of *Little Women* and in part by publication of a previously unpublished full-length sensational novel by the Concord author who experimented with so many genres and led a double literary life.

MS & LR JOURNALS » August

In the a.m. to McLeish. . . . He told us about Powell, who bought Wing books — 5th & 6th editions of unsaleable theological items . . . & cleared off all the dust-laden shelves of London. When we wanted to reach a high perch, McLeish said, "Don't be daft — stand on the folios" — so a pile of folios proved an excellent ladder.

We passed Goldschmidt's & decided to drop in again — a rare afternoon. L told him her Nicaragua story about Paul Heitz, her friend, the great Strasbourg publisher. "I was invited there for dinner," she recalled, "and was seated next to old Frau Heitz. In order to make me feel at home, she summoned up her recollections of the New World and cosily asked me, 'Was macht man ietzt im Nicaragua? — What's going on now in Nicaragua?' I wasn't quite sure just what Nicaragua was, but promptly responded, 'Ah, gans gut.' Goldschmidt had known Heitz well and loved the story. We bought a few more books from him, mostly scientific leftovers from his days in partnership with Ernest Weil. In between, tea was served, and Goldschmidt's young Dutch disciple Jacques Vellekoop was introduced to us. We left enthralled again with the great antiquarian — so enthralled that we walked the entire way back via Bond Street, Grosvenor Square, & Oxford Street, treading on air, carrying a bunch of roses we bought from a barrow.

After dinner the Festival — disappointing. . . . The illuminations on the river were lovely, however, & the sight of Big Ben & Whitehall bathed in light after these many years of darkness must bring joy to British hearts.

RETROSPECT Lawrence Clark Powell was at that time librarian at the William Andrews Clark Library in Los Angeles. He brought with him to London a marked copy of Donald Wing's *STC of English Books 1640-1700* and proceeded to snatch up everything his library lacked. As it turns out, this was a most astute operation — it pleased the British dealers of 1951 and it continues to gratify researchers today.

As for the charming and handsome Jacques Vellekoop, he hailed from South Africa and rose in time from discipleship to mastery, *becoming* E. P. Goldschmidt after the great man's death, and retiring in 1995. We would become quite friendly with him, returning to visit him in Old Bond Street for many years.

MS & LR JOURNALS » **August 5**

Yesterday a.m. took a complicated trip by Underground out to Hampstead to visit Norman — unchanged, though remarried & again a father. His shop is the grimiest, dustiest debris of horrors imaginable. Just the place where a Calderwood published by the Pilgrim Press in Leyden could be found for 5 bob. We didn't find the Calderwood, but we did find 7 small items, practically given away, & already have duplicate orders for 2 of them — so it was a profitable tho not an exhilarating jaunt.

After lunch we thought we'd take our chances at the Haymarket, & at the last minute got 2 cancelled seats in the stalls ($2.10 each) for *Waters of the Moon*, a charming play with Dame Edith Evans, Dame Sybil Thorndike, & Wendy Hiller. Tea was served to us during the "interval," & we sat very much a l'anglais, except for the American garbage we were still clutching from our Sterno lunch at the Cumb.

. . . today went to the National Gallery to pay our respects to some old favorites. . . . the Leonardo Virgin of the Rocks with its cold, cold light of blue ice — a rational light upon a most irrational scene. . . . The Londoners queue for the cinema, the red double-deckers chug by, the speakers shrill in Hyde Park. London is more crowded and wide awake than in other years. The fountains play in Trafalgar Square; oranges are for sale in the streets; eggs appear once a week; the shelled holes are being rebuilt or covered with false fronts; old wounds — some of them — are being mended, & so wags the world away.

MS & LR JOURNALS » **August 6**

This aft. to Fletcher in Wimbledon — royally received with a sumptuous tea shared by their black cat Timothy who sits on an armchair & eats scones. Much book talk: 1) Powell again, who spent his Guggenheim Fellowship buying Wing books for the Clark Library; 2) The "Ring" who corner the auctions; 3) The upper crust of American bookdom; 4) Captain Louis Henry Cohn, francophile founder of the firm of House of Books, Ltd., devoted to the moderns, scurrying to the South of France for a T. S. Eliot signature — etc., etc. Bought only 8 books, as Fletcher's prices are as elegant as Fletcher. But we had a jolly good time, didn't we, ducky?

MS JOURNAL » **August 9**

H. W. Edwards, a dealer who recently moved to London, is a stimulating person — 6 generations of Cockney behind him — firm & forthright in his opinions & full to overflowing with interesting talk. We are, it appears, "unique" in the trade — one in 60 million! "Women make the poorest book collectors." "Mrs. K. Gregory is a cutter-up of books." "The U.S.A. should be a colony of England — or vice versa." Meantime, we scoured the shelves & found several lovely books, including the Philip II Index *and* the Tagliente. Fletcher had a first (1524) & sold it for £90 this a.m. Ours is 1537 — we paid £20. Then had tea with Mrs. Edwards who, L tells me, had a butterfly tattooed on her ankle, which I missed.

RETROSPECT The 1537 Tagliente was an early edition of the first Italian writing book. In it the Italian calligrapher and writing master Tagliente included plates of writing instruments and specimens of various alphabets. The Philip II Index had been promulgated by the Spanish monarch in 1570 to forbid the printing, sale and circulation of heretical literature. Formulated by the bloody Duke of Alva, and printed in French, Flemish and Latin, it particularly opposed the spread of anti-Catholic works in the Netherlands. The clever H. W. Edwards would perhaps have commented: "You learn to write; then you must learn what not to write."

LR LETTER » **August 9**

Yesterday a.m. visited the very elegant Maggs on Berkeley Square, truly the most imposing house of rare books with odd volumes at 10,000 to 50,000 pounds but they're very sweet to us — let us look around in the dust heap & we did find 11 nice books — nothing astounding but all interesting.

I'm going to Ye Worshipful Company of Stationers at Stationers' Hall for my Martyn paper after much negotiation with the Hon. Beadle, Hon. Claaaark, Hon. Secretary.

The material I want to use is on exhibit & finally after several Downing Street communiqués they are dispatching the Hon. Secretary to be present this morning while I use some of the material.

RETROSPECT The Maggs "dust heap" was the enormous chamber on an upper floor where lesser material especially in French and English history was stored. Later on we would be emboldened to select books from the plush second floor with its vitrines and Dickens desk, and there one day we would find such treasures as Cyrano's voyage to the moon and a first of John Donne. But in 1951 we contented ourselves upstairs with less illustrious but not less intriguing volumes.

The visit to Stationers' Hall was interesting and fruitful. The Hall was located just to the left of St. Paul's Cathedral, and the two of us were escorted by Mr. Hodgson to what looked like the inside of a safe. Seated there, we examined the record books for references to L's printer, John Martyn, Printer to the Royal Society. As L wrote in a letter home: "He let us use most of the manuscript material, with the exception of one folio, screwed down in the exhibit. We did much searching & I really found very interesting, hitherto unknown material, which I shall eventually use in my Martyn paper." That Martyn paper appeared the next year in *The Papers of the Bibliographical Society of America* and was later reprinted in Rostenberg's *Literary, Political, Scientific . . . Publishing, Printing & Bookselling in England, 1551-1700*.

MS & LR JOURNALS » **August 13**
Yesterday Windsor. The gem of this sceptered isle. The Castle turrets rising white in a blue, blue sky. The military band playing airs while the bear-skins & red-coats marched, shouldered arms, & stood or champed. The green lawn & red geraniums — geometrically perfect. The white garden statuary. . . . People swarming about, chatting with the guardsmen. Oh, crisp, perfect jewel of a day set in green & red & blue & white. Then, to crown the setting, the band played "God Save the King" & the moving figures halted at attention. An 18th-century gem of an afternoon at Windsor Castle under an English sun. There is enough pageantry left in England to dispel the gloom of difficult living.

MS JOURNAL » **August 14**
At 6 we kept our appointment with the novelist Charles Morgan, to whom we had a letter of introduction. He stood beneath a portrait of himself throughout the interview and proceeded to enlighten and entertain us. He told us of his 9-months' lecture tour to the American

South — of the "great" Southern ladies who would not sing their Southern songs to an "outsider" until he proved himself an "insider" by referring to the Civil War as the War between the States. And he told us of his pleasant imprisonment in neutral Holland during the First World War, when he had a year with nothing to do but read & write. And then stories of Churchill galore. How he (Winston) allowed a young naval lieutenant to send 2 cruisers & 3 destroyers off Brest when German submarines threatened. Of meeting Churchill & Eden at the "Grand Night" of the Inns of Court. Of his son-in-law, the Marquis of Anglesey, & the latter's muniment room with its letters from Queen Elizabeth. . . . Of himself, whom he referred to casually as "the lion." Of myself as a "new" author, at which I was a bit annoyed. . . . His stories are little cameos in which he takes all the parts.

MS JOURNAL » **August 15**

Cambridge. We saw — for the first time — Trinity College Library. The first sight of that room is breathtaking — its noble, elegant proportions — the eye carried along the line of books & statues on either side of the room to the imposing statue of Byron. Statues at 2 levels — upper & lower — classical busts & busts of Trinity men. Book cases & book stacks — the black-&-white marble floor — the stained glass window over Byron. The details are unimportant — it is the sweep of the room that takes the breath away. And when you leave it you walk to the "Backs" with the weeping willows over the Cam. So beautiful, this university town. We have nothing comparable.

MS JOURNAL » **August 21**

Today we saw Canterbury. And that means that my head is filled with memories of a medieval town with narrow lanes & weavers' cottages — the Mercery, the Butchery — narrow passages that look to the fields or open on the canal-like Stour or into gardens whose scent is everywhere. It means my head is filled with the evidences of an ancient culture whose pottery and mosaic pavements have been unearthed among the debris of the blitz — the Roman Canterbury whose great wall still stands & whose atria have been so miraculously discovered beneath a tradesman's shop in Butchery Lane or in a street off the Parade. But above all it means that I am filled with thoughts of the Cathedral whose Gothic nave vaults to the sky & carries the heart soaring aloft with it.

I am filled with history. Again Becket is murdered in St. Benedict's Chapel on a dusky December evening; & once again the Black Prince is buried as he desired — his shields of war & peace beneath him. And yet again a ruby comes from Louis VII of France to adorn a crown that still survives. For I, too, was a Pilgrim to Canterbury in this late & distant age. Chaucer & his knight both rise before me & the prayers for Agincourt rise along with the Thanksgiving of 1942. For a thousand years in thy sight are but as yesterday when it is passed & as a watch in the night. I must not wax too poetical, but it is hard to refrain.

MS & LR JOURNALS » August

Half the library and bookselling world is here. . . . Emily Driscoll was here one night — we treated & we really had a very gemütlich clubby time — a colleague — but easy-going, good company & much good spirits.

To Fortnum & Mason to meet Weil for tea. While we were standing outside on Piccadilly, who came along but Karl Kup, who joined our party. So it was a sehr gelehrte quartet that sat tea-ing at Fortnum & Mason while L did the honors flawlessly. Weil, like a jolly old teddy bear, gave us a print for the office & we had ourselves a grand time. Kup told us Haraszti was in town, so we called him up & he spoke to us this morning. . . . too bad we didn't know earlier. This has been the best of the post-war trips. Lovely, varied, beloved England — au revoir.

RETROSPECT   In 1947 we were probably among the very few American dealers who had ventured to London in search of books. By 1951, "half the library and bookselling world" was there. The bookselling world was represented for us by Emily Driscoll whom we had first seen seated at a desk in Arthur Pforzheimer's bookshop where she doubtless leased space. Her speciality was from the beginning not books but autograph materials, and at that time she was scouting Napoleonica for the noted collector, Andre de Coppet. She developed quickly as a dealer in manuscripts, operating on her own in an office building on Fifth Avenue near the Library and later in fine quarters at the Architectural League. Through the years we came to know her well. She was extremely good looking in a kind of regal way; her charm overflowed; she was in every way an engaging and comfortable human being. Only in her later years after she moved to West Virginia did we lose touch with her. Before then she was often a close companion and always a welcome one. We touched base with her too whenever we went abroad at the same time.

Karl Kup represented the library world as Emily did the bookselling world. He was the prestigious chief of the Spencer Collection of prints and engravings at the New York Public Library. As for Haraszti, he was head of the Boston Public Library's rare book division. In the course of M's researches on New England personalities like Margaret Fuller and Louisa May Alcott, our paths had frequently crossed. We remember one occasion when he came to the Colonial Inn in Concord, Massachusetts, to dine with us and asked the waitress in his heavy Hungarian accent: "But ave you no pruns?" She probably had no idea what he wanted. As far as we know, he never got his prunes.

The bookselling world was also very much present in the purchases we made in 1951. One of them we found at the Orange Street establishment of Pickering & Chatto over which Dudley Massey then reigned. There we found John Dunton's *Religio Bibliopolae. The Religion of a Bookseller*, vindicating booksellers from the charge of being "a Pack of Knaves and Atheists." From our old supplier Bernard Breslauer we acquired a copy of the *Catalogus Librorum* issued by the late 17th-century London bookseller of "Little Britain," Robert Scott, whose 1674 catalogue offered to English readers the latest and the oldest from continental presses. Before selling this to the Folger Library, Leona would study it carefully, for it was to form an important source for her chapter on "Robert Scott, Restoration Stationer and Importer," destined to appear in the BSA *Papers* and subsequently in her compendium on English publishers.

And so our lives as writers and as booksellers came together in close connection. Both those lives were connected too with England, where we journeyed year after year in search of treasures to study and treasures to pass on.

1952

LR JOURNAL » **August 20**

London again — dear wonderful L that thrills us so. . . .

I do believe for the first time I feel exactly at home & as much at ease here as at home. . . . I adore London. . . . I won't in the winter when I look at the purchase price of our books — "Well, we paid $16.80 & sell it at $20 less 10% discount — you still made $1.20."

MS LETTER » **August 21**

We are right in the swing of London — almost as if we had never left. It's a grand old town, with its pearlies & bearded young men, & striped-suited barristers in homburgs & red double-decker buses & fruit barrows & flower sellers & all the color & noise of a great sprawling city plus the simple enchantment of the mews & lanes & alleys. Once you fall in love with London, you never fall out again.

LR & MS JOURNALS & LETTERS » **August 22**

Yesterday . . . to the Hampstead Horrors of Francis Norman, a reservoir of unconcealed & undisguised . . . rubbish gathered . . . by the angular, quiet "Francis" whose children use the books as darts & add to the general confusion & filth. The only addition is his little daughter who increases the pandemonium by picking up filthy books from the floor & throwing them around. What we found we literally "unearthed." Old bills & orders fly around everywhere — underfoot & overhead. Here you could really find a Bay Psalm Book for 70 cents — but we didn't. You walk knee-deep in books & climb a tottering ladder that sways among the piles & piles of books — & maybe one day we'll find a Grotius first up there.

RETROSPECT Visits to Norman would soon become even more hazardous as his young son matured sufficiently to be able to fire a water pistol at Papa's clientele, and we were always fortunate when he did not elect to throw a tome in our direction. His new wife punctuated our visits with beseeching calls for "FRAHNCIS — Hold the Baby!" Francis himself seemed ever more interested in selling his *Royal Geographics* at six pence a copy to the local gentry than in helping these two faithful American customers in their quest. Norman had never really recovered from the war's devastations. One day in the not too distant future we would be rewarded for our persistence, and find — not a Grotius first, not a Bay Psalm Book — but something almost as exciting.

LR & MS JOURNALS » August

Goldschmidt a dear — served us tea & climbed on chairs looking for our selections — quite a sight! — the patriarch of the trade climbing around for US! — rather for L who, according to Weil, enchants him. And G told us a lovely tale about Herbert Reichner for the benefit of R's ex-secretary-apprentice L.R. We knew of course that Reichner had edited the *Philobiblon* in Vienna before he emigrated to America. We knew too that Reichner's father had a plumbing establishment. Today G put it all together for us and described how he had visited the editor in Alt Wien and found him editing the *Philobiblon* while he was seated among, surrounded by, his father's toilets in plumber's paradise.

RETROSPECT One of the books in E.P.'s hands when he hopped down from a chair was the *Opera* of Celio Calcagnini. The calf-bound folio had been published in Basle by Froben in 1544 and it included an essay announcing for the first time that the earth rotated daily. This revolutionary statement had been enunciated by Calcagnini before Copernicus had made his world-shaking theories known. For $50 we purchased this pre-Copernican scientific bombshell from the great antiquarian of Old Bond Street.

MS JOURNAL » August 23

. . . To Seligman, where we saw Mr. Andrews & got. . . . another Castlemaine & another Sandford & prices not too steep. Digging is mighty hard, however, this year.

RETROSPECT It was fitting in 1952, when we were increasingly in love with England, that we purchased at the Cecil Court shop of Ernst Seligman 2 great English fête books. Sandford's handsome *History of the Coronation of . . . James II* brilliantly depicted the scenes in Westminster Abbey — the processions, regalia, enthronement of the monarch in 1685. The lavishly illustrated folio even included a plate of the banquet in the Abbey, a banquet consisting of 1,445 dishes such as pistach cream, stags tongues and cocks-combs. At the same time we acquired *An Account of*

His Excellence Roger Earl of Castlemaine's Embassy, From . . . James the IId . . . To His Holiness Innocent XI. When we left Cecil Court we carried with us, so to speak, the pageantry of England and of English history.

MS JOURNAL » **August 26**

Monday a.m. . . . to Grafton, where only Miss Hamel's hat showed the passage of time — not to mention the absence of books. We bought 2 after a search above & below stairs. It's true we found no rats this year — but no books either — loads of the old Marquis of Salsa books in vellum bindings still hanging around — but dull fare indeed. . . . Met dear Weil & his wife at the Royal Festival Hall, where we saw the Nutcracker ballet. The hall itself, a very modern affair, looks like an organ on the inside — the corps de ballet good but not exciting — saw Nathalie Leslie & John Gilpin do the Nutcracker & then a suite based on a Bizet symphony. Afterward, in Weil's chauffered car, to the Cafe Royal, where we "suppered" — pleasant talk — charming, dear sweet people.

. . . To Maggs, where we found the best stock in all of London. Wonderful rooms & wonderful books & Clifford as sweet as ever. We worked like Trojans on tottering ladders in the "cheap" room, & set aside over 25 books which will be priced tomorrow. Some extremely interesting ones — 16th- & 17th-century Continentalia.

RETROSPECT Two of the books we set aside in the so-called "cheap" room upstairs at 50 Berkeley Square would be right on course with 2 of our later collector-friends. A Bull issued in 1513 by Pope Leo X, the former Giovanni de Medici, concerned the nature of those montes pietatis or loan institutions that would one day form part of the economics collection amassed by our colleague Burt Franklin. A compendium of biographies of illustrious women compiled at the end of the 16th century by the Florentine humanist and exile, Ubaldini, would appeal eventually to our friend the feminist collector Miriam Holden. Franklin's collection would go, after his death, to Japan, Miriam's to Princeton. Our visit to Maggs in 1952 was already shaping connections.

LR & MS JOURNAL » **August**

London . . . is giving us weeks of uninterrupted happiness. I suppose it's the associations, the names, the streets, the signs, the antiquated customs, a certain splendor and stateliness that still abide & make it a great city with some pomp & circumstance. It is also the people — the affable "lift" operator who shows one the direction of "rugs and mats," the bus conductor who would have "lovie nip a bit faster." And this summer London is floodlit after 11 p.m. — Houses of Parliament, Big Ben, bridges, etc. — bathed in yellow light & Piccadilly looking almost like a miniature Times Square. The lights are on in London — at brief intervals.

MS JOURNAL » **August 29**

This a.m. to Herr Eisemann. We bought the tracts we had seen last year — 124 of them — German 16th & 17th century — some with nice woodcuts — $220 which brings up our total & brings down our average cost very nicely. He had a very profitable trip to America & was full of schmoos — not so Machiavellian any more. I'm very glad we clinched the purchase.

RETROSPECT Those tracts proved a howling success. They included little-known relations touching upon the German Reformation, rare news sheets concerning the various parties of the Thirty Years War, developments of the Hapsburg Empire, the Turkish wars, etc., etc. Eventually we sold every last one of them, mostly to our avid institutional customers: Newberry and Folger, the British Museum and the University of Basle, Harvard, Yale, the Library of Congress. They helped develop our interest in contemporary ephemeral throwaways that would shortly blossom into an abiding faith.

MS JOURNAL » **September 1**

Yesterday . . . High Wycombe. We . . . took the Green Line bus & it was a wonderful excursion. London yields reluctantly to the country & it was an hour — thru many provincial Main Streets — till we came to the country. Then the green hills of England repaid us, & at High Wycombe L sought out the Parish Church & cornered the curate just before a baptism to inquire about the grave of her printer Richard Baldwin, the location of whose remains is a bit questionable. It was a charming old church & then we trekked on to Hughenden, the manor of Disraeli, Victoria's great prime minister — so beautiful — among low lying hills & farmland — on a height

— shadowed by great, ancient trees. We saw his wonderful library, the drawing room, the vistas over the garden, the Victorian reliques — & enjoyed it all tremendously. The house is much as he left it — homey — lived in — & I could live there myself. Not so baronially sumptuous as Hatfield, but really lovely, & the setting a delight to the eye.

RETROSPECT It was Leona's deep interest in the Baldwins of the Old Bailey that drew us to High Wycombe. Richard Baldwin had been born there and was presumably buried there. He had been an ardent republican printer, and his wife Anne, who continued the business after his death, had not only supported but advanced his causes. The pair would form the subject of another Rostenberg article in the BSA *Papers* as well as a chapter of her book on 17th-century English printer-publishers.

MS JOURNAL » **September**

Yesterday a.m. to Stevens, Brown on Duke Street, where we did well, finding several nice 17th-century French items — and then to Myers where, at long last, we met the redoubtable Winifred. She is tops in the trade — one-time president of the English Booksellers' Association. She is also very charming and was as curious about L.R. & Inc. as we about her. We had always missed her in the past, she being away or in America when we were in London. Well, the curiosity, which was mutual, was gratified. She knew all about Leona and about my *Louisa May Alcott*. She would have driven us around the country had we called earlier.

RETROSPECT It was at Stevens, Brown that we finally succumbed to the Chaucer panel that adorns our wall today. The panel itself was part of a 16th-century church stall; the portrait depicts the poet in profile holding a rose. And today, hanging in our foyer, it greets our visitors as graciously as once forty years ago it greeted us on Duke Street.

It was at the New Bond Street Myers shop that we found a colleague who became more than a colleague — a true friend. At the time, Winnie Myers was carrying on the business originally established by her father. Her passion for manuscripts had not yet taken over, although soon she would abandon books for autograph materials. We first saw her seated in a tiny office at the rear of the shop. And there we sat huddled together, discussing our interests, so pleased that she was already familiar with much of our history, planting the seed of what would become a most companionable association every time our paths crossed.

MS JOURNAL » September

A visit to Penshurst, birthplace of Sir Philip Sidney. Crenellated Gothic towers of a rambling grey building dominating a lawn where sheep still graze & where the spirit of the English Renaissance still breathes its beauty on the air. . . . Went into the perfect gardens, where red flowers stand primly in place & marble benches & lily ponds make for perfection. . . .

Tea-ed in a little village inn. Then we walked the mile & a half back to the station. This was a high spot. . . . The wind swished thru the great trees & on either side the vistas of rising hills & farmland & grazing cattle surrounded us. Ivy & holly & pine needles at our feet — a Yost House at the end of the trek.

EVENING BEFORE DEPARTURE

It is evening in London & the lights are glowing outside the window & the double deckers are coursing in stately fashion up & down Park Lane. This is one of the few nights we have had for reflection. . . . Instead of going to Albert Hall, we decided to rest & so, as I write, a Schubert Impromptu is coming over the radio from Usher Hall in Edinburgh. It is a quiet evening & time to gather together the vari-colored threads of the past weeks in this most wonderful city. Books have been a bit disappointing — we have made no exciting finds — but we have replenished our stock, which was our purpose. And we have wandered through a London which, unlike the Londons of other years, was sunlit by day & floodlit by night. They are rebuild-ing London & it will rise as stately as before — with its checkered marble halls, its white stone. . . . I rejoice in the quality of this great city which, for all its greatness, is warm with friendship, kindly with courtesy, & full of the delight of the unexpected round every turn and down every lane. Even when you are not spectacular you have a grandness, & in my heart you will always be warmly alive.

RETROSPECT We did add a few exciting books to our shelves: the beau-tiful *Tapisseries du Roy* of 1679 depicting the elements and seasons; the

Salmon, *Polygraphice* in first edition of 1672 on drawing and engraving; in the area of science we bought a first of Humphry Davy's *Description of the Safety Lamp* from McLeish and a first of Wells' *Essay on Dew* from Dawson; at Murray Hill's we found the first English edition of Diderot's *Plan of the French Encyclopaedia* and a 1765 account of *The Trial of John Peter Zenger*, a milestone in the struggle for a free press.

MS JOURNAL » **September 8**

. . . We are in Paris — mad, colorful, vibrant, exciting, brash, noisy & EXPENSIVE Paris. We left Victoria — was it only yesterday? — at 11 a.m., took the train to Dover & boarded the *Invicta* for Calais. Sat in the first class tea lounge, tea-ing the whole way across as the cliffs of Dover grew dim & the coast of France loomed up. Then the Flèche d'Or to Paris. . . . The Scribe is a good hotel, but far from cheap. We dined in the grill room on lamb chops, French fries, peas & Camembert cheese (over $2.50 each). . . .

This a.m. had breakfast in our room — rolls & croissants, butter, jam & tea (about $1 each) & then began la vie Parisienne. Went to Clavreuil, where we bought very well — over 20 books — very cheap — ransacked his whole stock — & I washed on a cobbled court off the rue Saint-André-des-Arts while L snapped a picture....

Resumed business with a visit to Thiebaud (many interesting books). The latter is a picturesque antiquarian who assured L that her name was "bien connu" & who was not too shocked by our rusty French. . . .

. . . When it comes to food — oh my! We had hot chocolate & pastry on the Left Bank — super-delicious — but definitely — & tonight steak grillé au beurre — magnifique. However, every piece of butter, every cracker is entered on the bill & toted up — & it sure totes. We have spent! Prices exorbitant — of everything, apparently, but the books.

RETROSPECT In 1952 the proprietors of the two establishments — one on the rue Saint-André-des-Arts and the other on the rue des Ecoles — seemed to us more or less the same age. The paterfamilias Raymond Clavreuil, father of the future booksellers Jean and Bernard, resembled mine host of the inn, hail-fellow-well-met, breezy. He seemed always on the way to or from the hunt, although whether he hunted for foxes or for books, we never knew. He would welcome us every year until Jean took his place, and each year we would find books and pamphlets to augment our stock in French historical and literary works between 1500 and 1800.

Actually there was much that was foxlike about Raymond Clavreuil's colleague M. Thiebaud. Less welcoming, more suspicious, guarded by his 3 female assistants, he limited our searches to certain shelves and barred us from exploring upstairs areas. Nevertheless, from time to time we carried off a trophy from the bookstore on the rue des Ecoles, and almost always we carried off bread-and-butter books in the history of France.

During our short stay in Paris we tried to make our French seem more fluent by the extravagant use of dramatic gestures and head shakes. The dealers did not seem to mind. Most of them welcomed us with great pleasure and at every bookshop the firm name of Leona Rostenberg was "bien connu," a fact that pleased our international egos no end.

MS JOURNAL » **September 10**

. . . To the Left Bank, where we visited Desruelles & Leconte on the rue des Saints-Peres. Madame could show us little at the former — & the books were so tightly wedged in on the shelves that you needed a crowbar to extricate them. Bought only one book there — but that a lovely one.

Leconte was quite different — most eager to show & to please — & so, besides "jeting" the usual "coup d'oeil" on the open shelves, we examined the more prized items he brought in from the rear. We bought 6 books, including a beautiful copy of the first French Descartes.

RETROSPECT Several times during non-bookish Paris stays, we had visited the Invalides and gazed down at the tomb of the Little Emperor. Here lay, at last in peace, the man who had fought so many battles and changed the face and the history of Europe. Now, on the crowded shelves of Desruelles, we acquired the great folio by Le Jeune de Boullencourt that described the *Hostel Royal des Invalides* where Napoleon would one day be interred. Its splendid frontispiece showed an earlier ruler, Louis XIV, setting out for another war and at the same time ordering the building of the Hotel des Invalides. For us the volume encapsulated and dramatized much of French history.

From Leconte we purchased the same day the first French edition of Descartes' scientific landmark, the *Principes de la Philosophie*, in a superb copy, with frontispiece and plates, bound in vellum.

We learned early on that some of our most prized acquisitions would come from the tiny warrens in the rear of French bookshops where treasures were hoarded until the "moment juste."

LR & MS JOURNALS & LETTERS » September 12
Night before Sailing

This p.m., as has happened previously, by sheer accident we visited a splendid dealer & purchased a fine & unusually interesting collection of little 16th-century French historical tracts. And so, today crowned everything & we made a wonderful buy on our last day. First we went to Montmartre ... & then on to the Left Bank. ... Almost by chance we went to see a nearby dealer on our list. He saw we were interested in 16th- & 17th-century French material & asked us if we cared to look at more. He had a huge collection of lovely little French political tracts of the period — a cache of them. We bought 41 from him at 60 cents each!!! Wonderful! We are delighted. Our total is 456 books & we've spent just what we planned to.

RETROSPECT From time to time we had purchased French political ephemera — those unbound pamphlets that carry on-the-spot reports of battles and coronations, births and deaths, assassinations and reforms, alliances and hostilities. Now, with a collection of them to contemplate, we began to feel that, better than any lengthy tome, these brief contemporary accounts reflected history as it was happening. Their essence was timeliness and they were invested with an immediacy not to be found in later commentaries.

As the years passed, we would build up several large collections of these French political pamphlets that encapsulated their time. The first would be presented in our Catalogue 34 entitled *One Hundred Years of France 1547-1652: A Documentary History*. It would be sold en bloc. That collection would be followed by several others, all of them sold en bloc to various American institutions. Indeed we are still building up such collections and hoping to build more. But we trace the real beginning of our passion for such collections of French political ephemera to that fortuitous and serendipitous visit to the bookshop of Francis Roux-Devillas on the Rue Bonaparte on September 12, 1952.

MS JOURNAL » **September 12**

Paris is an effervescent, ebullient, flamboyant, exciting city. The contrast between the grandeur of its squares & the pettiness of its inhabitants bothers me a little. As an American, I resent having bus & taxi fares increase after 9:30 p.m. & a female overseer demand that I buy a ticket even before I sit down in the Tuileries Gardens. But that is Paris — the unpleasant part. We've seen much of its greatness & its beauty too. And carried a little of it away.

1953

LR JOURNAL » JULY

We are in Paris . . . a most volatile compelling city. To me the Left Bank represents much that must have been 17th-century Paris. . . . Never thought I'd bother at all to write but facing les toits de Paris it seems essential to do so since perhaps when I'm 81 (never will be) we shall wish to reflect upon a July in Paris when we bought books . . . when we tripped fairly carelessly through the avenues & rues de Dragon, St. Peres, Bonaparte, & up & down the Boul Mich & St. Germain — when we entered such dustbins as A. Picard & Cie or the truly fine quarters of M. de Nobele. Too bad about that fine entree book but 35,000 francs — trop, trop, trop cher! M's French is excellent — mine grows progressively more degenerate & garbled but impudently we go on.

. . . Paris — a city of the greatest & most tremendous contrasts — the Left Bank so incredible . . . so provincial . . . so petite ville — with all its fascinating streets & angles: rue du Dragon, rue des deux Colombieres, rue Bonaparte, rue Jacob, rue Danton, Boul Mich & all the old buildings falling apart & the busy priests & satisfied nuns walking in the shade & the drowsy cats & sleepy dogs & the patisseries & boulangeries, the maroquineries & the epiceries & all the flavor & smells . . . of Paris. It is an incredible city with its languid river rippling north & south having seen it all under the bridges — the magnificent Pont Alexandre, the Royale, Carrousel, Neuf, & the Cité & Notre Dame & the beautifully planned soft elegant Luxembourg Gardens — & the Cafe de la Paix & all the Americans.

MS JOURNAL » July 12

Yesterday — our first full day in Paris — we walked endlessly through the Left Bank — rue Bonaparte — rue des Saints Peres — cobbled walks, narrow streets, old, old houses jutting out grotesquely. Visited 3 dealers — Clavreuil, Roux-Devillas, & Vivien et Beurlet & have 40 books under our belts, averaging little more than $3 each — so we are pleased. In the evening walked along the broad & magnificent Champs Elysees to the Etoile, where the Arc de Triomphe was suddenly illuminated as we stood there. Nowhere else are there such radiant, wide, brilliant vistas — such life & vibrancy.

RETROSPECT Our 1953 visit to Roux-Devillas, where we had found the small pamphlet collection the year before, yielded us now Nicolas Aubin's provocative treatise entitled *Histoire des Diables de Loudun*. There the 17th-century Protestant minister had described the fascinations and the horrors of sorcery in Loudun when the Ursuline nuns had been "possessed" and the French priest Urbain Grandier had been charged with witchcraft and burned at the stake. Salem was a replay of one of the replays — Loudun. Its history intrigued us, as it did the novelist Aldous Huxley, whose *Devils of Loudun* played on Broadway. Many years later, when we visited Jacques Rosenthal near Munich and searched his decimated shelves, we would find the original decree that condemned Grandier to the flames. This *Factum pour . . . U. G. Prestre* was issued at Paris in 1634 and consisted of 12 pages. Here again was an ephemeral pamphlet that conveyed multum in parvo.

From Roux-Devillas also we acquired a copy of a 17th-century work by a male feminist — Poullain de La Barre, whose *De L'Excellence des Hommes, contre L'Egalite des Sexes* exposed the falsity of macho philosophy and upheld the equality of the sexes. On the same day we found a fine companion piece on Clavreuil's shelves — Pierre Petit's dissertation on the Amazons, those first feminists, organizers of the first feminist society. Petit's early salute to women would go before long to the ardent feminist collector Miriam Holden. She knew, and her great collection proved, that the Feminine Mystique of the twentieth century had had many antecedents.

MS JOURNAL » July 13

Today was a kind of unofficial pre-holiday in Paris. Tri-colors have begun to flutter from every window. The rain has stopped & sun pours down upon the leafy streets of the city while blue smocks, black friars, beggars & boulevardiers prepare for Bastille Day. Did we walk! All along the Boulevard St. Germain, the Blvd. St. Michel, the Seine, the bookstalls, the narrow streets, the old, old world that is Paris.

At Thiebaud's this a.m. got 18 more books — but tho he has books everywhere — even in the W.C. (where L found one) — he won't let you stray above the first floor. What scheming must go on behind his little blue eyes! Found a few more at Dommergues & Dorbon & collapsed at the Salon de The which we discovered last year on the Boul. Mich. And so we are really in Paris — and now for the fireworks.

In the evening we bussed & walked to the Gare du Luxembourg — Communist placcards of "Eisenhower Assassin" pursue us daily.

LR & MS LETTERS » **July 15**

. . . We are in the full swing of book buying. It is loads of fun making our wants known in French & conversing midst a rapid discharge of violent Gallican literary sallies. We bought some very nice items today, but, although there are many more rare book shops in Paris than in London, their stocks are small & the majority of the dealers are . . . difficile. They deny the existence of a single early printed book until one member of our firm has sneaked into the regions marked "prive" & there are always some attractive items. . . . Dealers offer no help whatsoever in the selection of books & let us struggle & pull if possible — but usually pas possible. When you remark to the proprietor, "C'est pas facile," the answer is quite simply, "Non, c'est pas facile, Madame." Also, the 12-2 lunch hours are taken very seriously & we are serenely kicked out just as the chase becomes hot, & have to return "après deux heures."

Picard, on the rue Bonaparte, *looked* like a real possibility — crammed with calf & vellum backs but upon close inspection they turned out to be real mediocrities — *Telemaque* — Orace — Life of St. Somebody — 18th-century flavorless material.

RETROSPECT How wrong we were! It was not until we returned home and examined our Picard purchases carefully that we realized we had hit a jackpot. Among our selections from his stock was a collection of 8 17th-century French pamphlets, most of them concerned with Franco-Spanish politics. One of them was entitled: *Copie de la Réqueste*

Présentee Av Roy d'Espagne . . . sur la descouverte de la cinquiesme Partie du Monde, appellée la terre Australle, incogneue, & des grandes richesses & fertilite d'icelle. It had been written by Pedro Fernandes de Queiros and printed in Paris in 1617. As we read the text, our heartbeats accelerated. When we studied our find we learned that the author, Senor Queiros, had been a celebrated Portuguese navigator in the service of Spain who had sailed from Peru to the "Terre Australe." He was convinced he had discovered the Antarctic Continent which he named Australia del Espiritu Santo and claimed for the Spanish Crown. Now he was asking for funds to prosecute further discoveries.

It was hard to price this ephemeral treasure whose few pages encompassed a newly found land. The eight pamphlets together had cost us $2.90. When we met our colleague Carola Payne, specialist in voyages and travel, at a local association meeting, we mentioned our Queiros to her, along with the price we had tagged it — $250. Carola grabbed it. Today, if it ever appears on the market, that price would be inflated to many thousands. In the "Terre Australe," Queiros had found riches. At the end of the rue Bonaparte we had found riches of a different kind.

LR & MS LETTERS » July 17-18

. . . Our days are just filled with books & exploration — we traverse one small street after another with jutting roofs & gay flowered windows, with ancient churches, gesticulating market women, cats, rotting vegetables, nuns with wing collars, monks, priests in flowing capes, old women in black even to their black cotton stockings, women clutching their long loaves of bread, motorcycles, salons de thé, brasseries, print dealers, binders, booksellers — & all the smells & life of Le Quartier Latin. It is so completely stimulating, provincial, messy & exciting.

Today we found some excellent books, particularly at one shop where we had never bought before, & the dealer requests "nous reviendrons demain pour des autres." The majority of dealers have modern books, but we "Bonjour" at all & love every step. . . . Rain & sun every day but it doesn't matter — the spirits soar & the quest continues.

(Later): . . . we found another collection of French tracts similar to if not better than the collection we found last year — over 40 of them.

RETROSPECT This second collection of French political pamphlets was found at 19 rue de Tournon in the shop known as Thomas-Scheler. In 1953 it was operated by Lucien Scheler himself, distinguished poet and scholar. In later years the presiding genius would be Bernard Clavreuil, son of Raymond, brother of Jean Clavreuil. Each year we would visit the shop on the rue de Tournon where we would find many highlights. This year, in addition to the collection of tracts, we selected the beautiful mid-16th-century emblem book, Cousteau's *Pegma*, as well as a volume of military plates by the distinguished 17th-century Italian engraver Della Bella. As for the collection of French political pamphlets offered by Scheler, they were all dated 1559 or 1560 — edicts and ordinances promulgated by Francis II, covering the varied phases of his rule: the sale of wines, salt and spices, the priest and the soldier, governors and hospitals, money and second marriages, royal officers and the reformation of the church. The price of the pamphlet had risen — these averaged $1.70 each. We would sell most of them to Folger in a small collection. How we would like to buy them back!

MS JOURNAL » July 20

. . . In the afternoon we had wonderful luck, just chancing to go into an unknown dealer's — Magis on the rue Guenegaud. There we found just our sort of books — 16th century French — interesting — including 27 17th-century French tracts — & departed with our pacquet joyously.

RETROSPECT Like the Scheler establishment, Magis' shop would become an annual imperative for us. Our first view of Jean-Jacques Magis' premises was intimidating. Books were piled everywhere and his bookshelves soared to the ceiling. Without a ladder it was impossible to view the upper layers. Actually we stood on folios, a cascade of books falling on our heads from time to time, while Monsieur Magis cocked an eye at us from his desk. It soon developed that this young mustachioed monsieur had a passion for French political history which we shared, and as the years passed our relations with him grew very cordial. He would move later on to enormous quarters on the rue Saint-Andre-des-arts, near the Librairie Clavreuil. We would follow him there of course, and one day he would even venture West and pay us a visit in Manhattan. In 1953 we garnered from his rue Guenegaud shelves twenty-seven French tracts of 1612–15 at 60¢ apiece, along with several other works on sixteenth- and seventeenth-century French wars and government.

From an early history of Joan of Arc to theories on education by a member of the Enlightenment, we had ranged in our Paris purchases. All told, we bought more than two hundred books during our stay in the City of Light, at the incredible average of $3.75 each. From the Hotel Lutetia we had walked almost everywhere, to the Luxembourg Gardens and the Tuileries, past ancient statuary, playing fountains, beds of begonia, petunia and mignonette. We had found dealers new to us who would be our faithful suppliers for years to come. We had rejoiced in Paris en plein air — a Paris we carried off in our hearts.

MS JOURNAL & LR & MS LETTERS » July 24
We were greeted by all & sundry at the Cumb. London seems to be brighter than ever — more food & fewer restrictions. . . . Most of the traces of Coronation are gone, but here & there you see remnants of banners & festive signboards, and the spirit of this island seems still infected with some of the joie de vivre. However, we Americans are completely disliked & now held in the greatest opprobrium because of the Rosenberg case. . . .

Yesterday we visited the affable Messrs. McLeish & got a few nice books, though their shelves are sorely depleted; Thorp — very few books — & the glum proprietor as glum & uncommunicative as ever; an afternoon audience with Herr Goldschmidt who really worked for us through all his old cards, was a darling, but looks terrible. His assistant worshipped at the foot of the temple & so did we, though L asked him to erase a 10/6 mark from a book he priced for us at $20. Got interesting humanism from him as always. . . .

RETROSPECT The warmth and affection that had flowed to American visitors from the British in the years that followed the war were now perceptibly diminishing. One reason for this may well have been the Rosenberg case — the trial of Ethel and Julius Rosenberg by the United States Government for espionage on behalf of the Soviet Union. That trial and the defendants' subsequent execution, as well as the American fear of the Communist bogeyman, would cast a pall upon European-American attitudes for quite some time.

As for our revered humanist-scholar E. P. Goldschmidt, he would die the following year, and his firm would pass into the extraordinarily capable hands of his disciple Jacques Vellekoop. Meanwhile we recall that one of the books we selected from his "old cards" in 1953 was an unusually interesting Spanish guide to the Escorial written in 1589 by Juan de Herrera, architect to Philip II of Spain. Apparently the plates depicting the Escorial were not part of the volume but were sold separately to visitors and sightseers. The copy we bought from Goldschmidt was not accompanied by the plates, but it did have a most provocative purchase inscription at the end, a statement in Latin that the work had been acquired at the Escorial in 1614 by a collector who boasted that for 30 realis he had bought the 11 plates as well as the guide book. Our copy would go to the Avery Architectural Library at Columbia, where it would continue to tell its intriguing tale of sightseers and collectors and the passing centuries.

MS JOURNAL » **July 24**

This a.m. had breakfast with Nat Ladden & schmoosed long & furiously re books. Then to Maggs where Mr. Clifford was as sweet & fumbling as ever & where we had the run of the Emporium, climbing ladders & gathering 17 babies. Lunched with Emily Driscoll & Ruth Collis of Stevens, Brown at the Welbeck — most enjoyable — & then back to Maggs to conclude our deal & on to Davis to start another. Bought a few beauties from the latter, who seems to feel some guilt at his shabby treatment of us, & are to return to Maddox Street on Wednesday.

RETROSPECT Nat Ladden, co-proprietor of Maurice Inman, Inc., in Manhattan's East 50s, catered to a kind of carriage trade in lavish books, journeyed to London every year, and stayed at the Cumberland just about when we did. We enjoyed his companionship, swapped stories about books and book people, and shared a warm friendship for many years.

The Maggs foray of 1953 added to our shelves several notable works: a 16th-century dialogue on political theory by a French Renaissance scholar; the writings of Olympia Fulvia Morata, an Italian Renaissance feminist, which would naturally go to our 20th-century American feminist friend Miriam Holden; and, most significant of all, the 1522 first Latin edition of Luther's acrimonious reply to Henry VIII. Leona would offer this Reformation highlight to the Reformation collector Clinton Bebell, informing him: "We have just returned from abroad and can offer you the following rare Luther item. We have not offered this work elsehere and shall welcome hearing from you. . . . We searched diligently for Luther items and they are really becoming difficult to obtain." This Luther item was dispatched immediately.

The reference to Davis' "guilt" and "shabby treatment" relates to the devaluation of the pound. Our last purchases from Davis had been made prior to that devaluation, but the pound was devalued before we actually paid for our acquisitions. Since they had been purchased at the old rate, we felt the compunction to pay at the old rate instead of the new. At the time, Davis wrote us a letter expressing his overwhelming gratitude and stating that he would never forget what we had done. Apparently a cold winter in London reduced his gratitude, for Davis did indeed forget. His promise to search out books for us in Italy came to nothing. And as for items selected at his shop on Maddox Street, his prices soared for the most part beyond our means.

MS JOURNAL » **July 25**

This a.m. — a Saturday — we did the Charing Cross section — the Cecil Court boys: Seligman & Low, & in the afternoon Marks & Joseph. Got a total of 10 books after much backbreaking effort. Joseph, the elder, still sports his bowler & persuasive manner & has added an extremely natty vest to the ensemble. Low's beard is bushier than ever & his books even duller. Seligman was away, but Mr. Andrews is as bent as ever upon keeping order in the shambles of Cecil Court.

RETROSPECT Of the 10 books our "backbreaking effort" yielded from Cecil Court, one was an 18th-century item, two 17th-century and seven 16th-century. Today the outcome of a visit to the Charing Cross area would probably consist of nine 20th-century reprints and one 19th-century first. As for David Low, he would move later on to Emmington Chinor near Oxford, to a charming house once owned by the English prime minister Clement Attlee, and would write a delightful autobiographical reminiscence entitled *With All Faults*.

MS JOURNAL & LR & MS LETTERS » July 29-30

This a.m. ransacked Davis & got 17 books — not cheap — but some really *very* fine. So we're pleased, though we could wish there had been 3 times as many. Got another Cellini, *Vita*, the Beze *Icones*, etc.

. . . To Myers — got a couple of books & a peepshow of the Thames Tunnel. . . . Picked up one real rarity sandwiched in with a lot of travel books, which she gave us for 10 bob ($1.40). . . . Winnie asked us, "How long have you been in business?" When we told her, she replied, "Amazing, I thought years & years because you are so well known." We were duly pleased.

RETROSPECT   We were more pleased with some of our purchases. The 10 bob item we found sandwiched in "with a lot of travel books" at Winnie's was the first Italian work published in England. It was a life of Charlemagne by the Italian resident in England, Petruccio Ubaldini, and our copy of this rarity went to Yale.

As for Davis, we worked off some of our initial disappointment by the purchase of two glorious fete books. One was the *Ercole in Tebe* of 1661, a play illustrated with handsome plates celebrating the nuptials of Cosimo III, Grand Duke of Tuscany, and his unwilling bride Margherita Louisa, daughter of the Duke of Orleans. The other was a fine folio printed in Moscow in 1762 with text in Russian and German, hailing the coronation of Catherine II as Empress of Russia. This would go to the Metropolitan Museum of Art.

We also found, among the 17 books harvested from the visit to Davis' establishment, two other books remarkable for their beauty. The Beze *Icones* of 1580 was a distinguished portrait and emblem book of the Renaissance, bound in full green morocco stamped with roll work of gilt concentric circles. Boissat's *Le Brillant de la Royne* of 1613 was a biographical study of the Medici family embellished with Medici portraits; its engraved title-page depicted a diamond pendant suspended from a fleur-de-lys. Where today could we assemble such treasures from a single day's explorations?

LR LETTER » **August 1**

. . . Yesterday a.m. we visited the mercurial Mr. Davis from whom we purchased a total of 25 books — including those from our first visit.

He's très difficile but since I'm not writing a history of London bibliophilic personalities & am only interested in acquiring books, I don't care. We purchased some highly interesting material at high prices but we need books — they are all unusual & I know in time we shall do well.

Fri. . . . I forgot to tell you that the three of us (L, M, Nat Ladden) dined at Simpson's last night. It was very good on a pre-war basis & we had a very enjoyable time — took our time & later walked along the Embankment, Whitehall & through Bird Cage Walk to the palace — taxied home & had coffee in the lobby. . . .

We entrained to Newbury, Berkshire, where, upon arrival, a chauffeured car met us & took us to H. W. Edwards. He has a small house, a separate book house & grounds. . . . They grow everything, have 2 hot-houses, a mad disarray of flowers & English lavender in profusion of which Mrs. E. gave us a generous picking. We were regaled with low and high tea. . . . Edwards is an interesting, out-spoken gent who regards Americans as semi-savages & denizens of a remote world, but enjoyable to a degree. He had some books but his prices were exorbitant — so after all the rush, we only purchased 4.

MS JOURNAL & LR LETTER » **August 4-5**

. . . To Albert Hall for an all-Tchaikovsky program. . . . Sat in a box overlooking the standees ($1.40 each). Sir Malcolm Sargent con-ducted. Had coffee & biscuits during intermission . . . & gloried in it all. They do this sort of thing better than we & with more enthu-siasm, I think. Our lovely London — where the bus drivers leave their busses to help mummy with the pram. So wonderful!

MS LETTER & JOURNAL » **August 5**

This a.m. . . . went to Quaritch (prices exorbitant), where we saw many of the books we had bought in Paris for about one quarter of what Quaritch asked — so we are well satisfied. . . .

. . . After lunch to Gurney, where we hit a fine cache — got 14 fine & interesting books, including a first of Spinoza bound with several replies & a lovely Herberstain on the Muscovites. Grand pickings after a general dearth.

A Mr. Lyon, who has been in business only a year, called & took us to his place in the neighborhood (around Campden Hill). He had very few books tho we did get one for which we have a duplicate order — along with tea & a drive back to the hotel.

We are well satisfied. Score is now 410 books — & we had aimed at 400. We can be content. Gurney was a surprise & a windfall at this moment. He had a very interesting stock. AND WE HAVE TOO.

M. and L. in the office, 1953

RETROSPECT At the time we visited Richard D. Gurney he had assembled a general stock. Later he specialized in medicine, science and technology, and our visits to him became fewer. The Herberstain we selected during our first visit to him was an illustrated 16th-century travel book to Russia and ranks as one of the great sources for the Muscovite Empire.

On the other hand, while our visits to Gurney decreased, our brows-ings at Dick Lyon's increased. He had — still has — a small house at Selwood Terrace in the Campden Hill area and he eventually special-ized in illustrated books and early French and Italian novels and trea-tises that appealed to us. His good taste was reflected in his stock, and we were always able to find a few items that intrigued us at Selwood Terrace. He pronounced his name not LY-ON but LAHN in a very British drawl. He himself was a languid English gentleman who seemed somewhat enigmatic to us.

LR & MS JOURNALS » **August 8** » *Day of Departure*

Ninety percent of the trade was never more cordial & we felt most welcome & appreciated here, from the glorious heights of Maggs to the lowly depths of a Faginesque cellar off Holborn Place where books live in squalor and disorder.

And so it is over . . . This afternoon the boat train & a week from today — Manhattan & the Bronx. Sic transit. In the end is a new beginning.

1954

LR LETTER » **August 14**

It all seems incredible but we are here, each in one piece & each extremely ecstatic over the marvels of air flight. . . . The flight was really a tremendous experience & I am very happy we did it as all fears were dispelled and London is just an odd 17 hours from home. We reached Sydney, Cape Breton Island, at 11:30 p.m. — had coffee there (after a meal en route) & then began the big hop, at 19,000 feet, crossing the ocean & arriving at Prestwick, Scotland at 2 p.m. English time (9 U.S. time). . . . Then on to London arriving at 4:30, actually 11:30 our time. Just imagine. And the boat takes 7 days. . . .

Upon arriving here (Cumberland) we received a cordial welcome from all — "Luggage Master" to Madam the Housekeeper — & are ensconced in a nice room overlooking Hyde Park. Just think — in our room we found flowers of welcome from Winnie Myers & several letters, one of which tickled me no end, from editor of the English Bibliographical Society, Librarian of Cambridge, accepting my article on Nathaniel Thompson. . . . We both whooped barbarically in the Cumberland lobby. . . .

LR LETTER & MS JOURNAL » **August 16**

. . . Saturday's book hunting began with a bang. We bought 54 books & among that number some beauties — a few were extremely reasonable, although we paid healthy prices for many. In the afternoon Gurney, a nice chap, served tea & showed us interesting material. . . .

On Sunday we were dined & wined by the combined English & American book forces. Winnie Myers called for us in her 1938 Austin which holds 4 people, took us for a picnic in Richmond Park, & we sight-saw en route.

Later to Strawberry Hill, the celebrated pseudo-Gothic castle of Mr. Horace Walpole, Sion Palace, the Palladian estate of the Duke of Burlington — & Becky Sharp's domicile. Met Frances Hamill & Margery Barker at the English Speaking Union & dined there at their invitation. The latter very sweet & pleasant — the former queen regent of the trade. Wormsers — Dick & Carola — came later, quite high, but lots of fun — we enjoyed being with them.

There is something that distinguishes book dealers from most other business & professional people — & whatever it is, we like it.

. . . London is much better — bacon & eggs for breakfast — sweets, meats — everything off ration, & life is easy once again.

RETROSPECT The "interesting material" shown us and sold to us by Richard Gurney included two works of far more than ordinary interest. One was a congratulatory tribute on the marriage of Henry VIII and Anne Boleyn by Luther's arch-opponent Cochlaeus, in first edition of 1535. This went

L. and Winifred Myers at Strawberry Hill, 1954

to the Newberry. Another, also in first edition, was Campo's superbly illustrated Renaissance chronicle on the city of Cremona. Beautiful in itself, the work was distinguished for other reasons also. It included a plate by Leonardo da Vinci depicting the portrait of Massimiano Sforza, the original of which is lost. It also contained two maps signed "David De Lavde Hebrevs Cremona Incidi," the first Jewish engraver associated with map-engraving. Fascinated by the Judaic interest of this Italian history, Joshua Bloch, the learned curator of the New York Public Library's Jewish Division, eagerly bought the Campo.

In August 1954 some Americans had already gathered in London prior to the biennial International Congress scheduled to be held in Vienna. Naturally the current president of the Antiquarian Booksellers Association of America was much in evidence. Frances Hamill of Chicago was the partner of the attractive and genial Margery Barker. Frances was a bit of a martinet, bent upon keeping the sometimes unruly American dealers (including us) in order. Dick Wormser was the paterfamilias of the Association. He knew its Constitution by heart and quoted it frequently. However, his strict allegiance to regulations did not interfere with his sense of humor. He had recently married the dealer

Carola Payne, widow of the rare book dealer Alfred Payne. He could be counted on for comments ranging from acerbic to hilarious, and besides keeping us all in parliamentary order he kept some of us in stitches.

LR LETTER » August 18

. . . We've been so busy that time is at a premium. We've made a record in book purchases — 144 in 3 days! . . . Davis has moved into a perfectly charming private house off Bayswater Road, in Orme Square, with garden, pool, fountain, fish, & stupendous books. . . . Bought over 20 including a first of Newton, & some lovely Renaissance stuff.

We've been heartily congratulated for our Renaissance Catalogue by Davis. McLeish called it "the very best I've seen in years," & Clifford Maggs told me in his lispy, wispy English, "It was wonderful." Maggs is an incredible place — a superb time ascending & descending ladders.

RETROSPECT Until his final move to Hampstead, Davis' establishment at Orme Square would attract us now year after year. This year, our 20 purchases included a verse play of 1594 by the Italian pioneer actress and scholar, Isabella Andreini, "first actress of Europe." This would of course go to Miriam Holden. A Doni, *Libraria* of 1550, the first Italian national bibliography in first edition, would go to the University of Kansas. And our Davis haul also included the first edition of Sir Isaac Newton's *Opticks*, a monumental work on the subject that became a landmark in the history of science.

Besides praise from McLeish we carried off from him a most curious 17th-century English work extolling women warriors during the English Civil Wars and entitled *Joanereidos: Or, Feminine Valour; Eminently discovered in Western Women, At the Siege of Lyme*. And, in addition to Maggs' encomia we acquired from 50 Berkeley Square a printed letter from Henry VIII defending his stand against Luther in 1523 before his breach with the church, along with another fine feminist item, the collected writings of Hroswitha of Gandersheim who would join Isabella Andreini on Mrs. Holden's shelves.

MS JOURNAL » **August 18**

A wonderful day at Vellekoop's — erstwhile Goldschmidt's — such a young man — & such a stock. He took us over the premises from top to bottom — showed us his improvements, etc. (G. had never had a basin with running water). A very smart young man — turned over the place to us — took us to Brown's Hotel for a complete & elegant lunch — & we bought 27 items from G's old stock, bringing the grand total to 171 after only 4 days of London book buying. A record. After our day with that very aesthetic young man in the black check suit & yellow suede shoes, named Jacques Vellekoop, we called it a day — as it was.

RETROSPECT After Goldschmidt's death, Jacques Vellekoop inherited his establishment and the premises at 45 Old Bond. Jacques quickly made his own preferences and personality felt. The former expressed itself in the modern bathroom; the latter in the red and black wallpaper that now adorned one room, as well as in the electric adding machine.

At the time of his death, Leona wrote a brief recollection of E.P. for the *Antiquarian Bookman*. It evoked the following poignant response from the Cecil Court bookseller David Low, who characterized her reminiscence as a "flavored memory of E.P.G." "It brought back memories of his inimitable little anecdotes in that first-floor room. I do understand how your visits to London will be blanker henceforth. He used to tell me how you were his favourite 'in statu pupillo.'"

In 1954 the Goldschmidt stock was naturally more "flavored" of Goldschmidt than of Vellekoop. We bought from him Languet's great enunciation of the contractual theory of government between ruler and subjects, as well as a rare Shelley association item concerned with the statue of Ozymandias that may have inspired the poet's celebrated sonnet. In later years, Jacques Vellekoop would expand his humanistic stock with many great and lavish works.

MS JOURNAL » **August 22**

At Harding's we selected about 30 fine books — found them helter skelter in piles of books upstairs, but Wheeler told us to come back so he'd have time to check & price them. We went to Fortnum & Mason for tea — but even crossed fingers did not work. He priced everything high — I think just because we had selected them. Anyway, we took 11 items — too bad.

. . . In the afternoon to Weil. Still a darling — we sat in his study with a fire going, & schmoosed & looked — got some very fine items including a Galilei, Scamozzi, & the Estienne Frankfurt Book Fair — not cheap, but good. He told us much about Goldschmidt, Davis, cats — Mrs. Jepson (a partner of Davis) keeps hers in a portable hat box; Goldschmidt fed his fish from the 4th floor & chicken from Brown's below, giving it a false idea of natural history — etc., etc. A wonderful tea in between the books — open sandwiches: tomato, salmon, egg, cheese — a marvelous cheese cake — the 2 Mrs. Weils — the elder thought we looked familiar, but her main contribution to the entertainment was a prolonged cough. The cat very dignified. All as always. Really lovely — English book buying at its best & brightest. He's taking us out for lunch Thursday.

RETROSPECT Book gossip is commonplace in all countries among all booksellers. Since Davis and Goldschmidt were such unique characters in the trade, chitchat about them was always of the greatest interest. Weil's reference to Mrs. Jepson did not surprise us, since we had met that lady at Orme Square and had already been introduced to her cat Ginger who relaxed in her hat box. We also knew that she was a fine pianist and a very close friend of Irving Davis. We also knew of the many vagaries of E.P.G. and had been frequently told of his generous estimate of our scholarship. Naturally we did not object to hearing it again.

We were delighted with our purchases from Weil, never having dreamed we would own first editions of Galilei's *Systema Cosmicvm*, one of the 3 great masterpieces of modern astronomical literature, and of Estienne's celebrated treatise of 1574 on the Frankfurt Book Fair. Little did we dream also that 6 years later Madeleine would inaugurate the first New York Antiquarian Book Fair which, like the Frankfurt variety, would be repeated annually and enjoy an international reputation.

MS JOURNAL & LR LETTER » August 24

. . . Betty Woodburn returned our telephone call. We hied ourselves to the Hyde Park Hotel & dined with them amid the elegancies of a Frenchified maison in Knightsbridge. They're a darling couple & we're very fond of them. Schmoosed in their gorgeous

Edwardian room about the book hunt & Keith's work on a naval hero & enjoyed it all.

. . . Yesterday a.m. went to Stationers' Hall where we received a warm welcome from the Beadle of the Company & repaired to the safe. We did quite some research & found very good material. Our enthusiasm was somewhat chilled by the damp vapors rising from the original Roman Castra beneath & the bombed-out areas surrounding the Hall. It is directly below St. Paul's & when we arrived for one brief moment the sun flirted with Ludgate Hill & it was a splendid glorious moment to feel an English sun as St. Paul's chimed 10.

RETROSPECT Our meeting with Elisabeth Woodburn and her husband Keith Robertson developed into a long-lasting friendship. Over the years we would visit them often at their lovely Booknoll Farm in Hopewell, New Jersey. Betty specialized in horticulture, herbals, gardening, and books about the home, wine and cookery. Keith was the author of many successful books for boys including the Henry Reed series. We enjoyed their garden, their home, their cookery, their books, and especially themselves. Betty was extremely active in the Antiquarian Booksellers Association of America of which she became president. Before her untimely death she bequeathed a generous fund to the Association.

MS JOURNAL » August 26
Last night spoke to Miss Pitcher of the Folger on the phone — most complimentary — has wanted to meet us — invited us for tea Saturday at her flat on Curzon Street.

RETROSPECT Although we were well acquainted with the Folger Shakespeare Library of Washington, D.C. — indeed they had ordered 32 books from our Renaissance catalogue — we had never met the presiding genius of Acquisitions, Eleanor (better known as "Molly") Pitcher. She was a woman of tremendous charm and beauty and had great taste and enthusiasm for early printed books. Each year "Molly" visited London where she was received as the Belle of the London Book Trade. When she entertained us in her Curzon Street flat, she invited us to go all through the Folger. We preferred she would go all through Rostenberg's, so we asked if she would not visit us up north in the Bronx. Despite her reply: "Oh, you're way up, aren't you?" — she did indeed arrive there for lunch — and for books. The Folger, even after "Molly's" death and the retirement of her able successor Elizabeth Niemyer, would remain a faithful customer.

LR LETTER » **August 30** » *Hotel Sacher, Wien*

We left London (Cumberland) at 7:30 & arrived at airport by 9. Flight left London at 9:40 — a superb plane — & I was snoozing a bit when the hostess announced: "We are descending." I thought we had just hit France & we were at Zurich. It is incredible. Took 12 minutes to cross the Channel. We got out at Zurich — a wonderful airport — reembarked, had excellent lunch at 19,000 feet & arrived at Vienna at 2:05. The aerodrome here was in horrible contrast to Zurich & London — all the environs had been completely bombed & the shambles remain. Our first taste of the outskirts consisted of bombed buildings far worse than London in 1947 — decay, poverty, & military police with ready tommy guns.

Our room at Sachers could house the remainder of the Hapsburg dynasty & is incredible — a crystal chandelier — a divan, vanity, desk, table, chairs & huge portraits. If we had more time we'd call in the Stadt Herr Cosmographer to chart its dimensions. The Association sent us an exquisite bouquet . . . and a wonderful box of Altman & Kuhne candies. . . .

Reception of ILAB in the Baroque Room of the Landhaus, presided over by a member of the Austrian Senate. . . . Welcoming addresses in English, French & German — vin d'honneur. . . .

LR LETTERS
MS LETTER & JOURNAL » **August 31-September 1**

After 2 days in Vienna our impressions: Europe in limbo — Wien in transition — imperial, regal, monstrous architecture in decay — stone houses dilapidated & frequently riddled with bullet holes. Military police in evidence. East plus West. The Russian soldiers are everywhere but completely withdrawn & uncommunicative. It is a captive city, the prey of 4 nations. We're in the international zone — this month headed by the Russians. Saw Stalinplatz with the Red Star & pictures of Lenin & Stalin much in evidence. You often see Russian street names here. The major art centers have been completely obliterated: e.g., Goering requisitioned the entire Lichtenstein Collection & it has disappeared. The parks, squares & buildings are neglected — the opera house in a state of reconstruction & the composite picture is that of postwar devastation & shame. The city is one of the greatest contrasts: Renaissance, Hapsburg, Baroque, 19th-century dullness, Karl Marx Community houses & Russian occupation coupled with delightful cafe life, beggars, Tyrolean costumes and superb apfel strudel!

MS JOURNAL & LR LETTER » August 31-September 2

On Monday a.m. the entire congregation assembled outside the Antiquariat Heck & were taken in buses on a sightseeing trip through Wien to Schonbrunn. Schonbrunn was awful — nothing but gilt & large porcelain stoves — a succession of gaudy rooms with mementoes of Maria Theresa, Franz Joseph & L'Aiglon. Then an elaborate lunch al fresco — beer — kalte zunge — griesnockerlsuppe — tafelspitz — strudel.

We took the subway back to town — abandoned by the buses (kleinisch-keit Europeenne) & convened for a general assembly. We sat with the American delegation where our flag waved & we all chauvinistically greeted each other: Geoffrey Steele . . . & wife, Laurence

ILAB Congress, Vienna, 1954

Gomme, Frances Hamill, Betty & Keith. . . . Heard the addresses in French & English. Awful to understand both. Much discussion about petty points (to us). Had dinner at the Cafe Mozart with the Robertsons & Laurence Gomme & then to our room. They got hysterical at our high ceilings, lamps, mirrors, chandelier & general acreage.

This a.m. was "free" — so after our elegant breakfast in our elegant chamber we strolled forth — bought 11 books from Gilhofer & 2 from Lechner's window, including some lovely woodcut books.

. . . Altogether we have bought 50 books in Vienna including a fine windfall from Herr Hinterberger who snorts around & pushes his big belly in front of him & was overwhelmed by all the orders. It was he, we discovered, who had sold the Tin Mining Ordnung to Weil — & we bought it from the latter — so we have found the source of the source. Also bought from Heck on the Karntnerstrasse — some very nice items.

RETROSPECT Of all the Viennese booksellers, Herr Hinterberger was the most colorful. Probably suffering from some asthmatic disorder, he huffed and puffed as he dashed about, surprisingly agile for a man of his rotundity. He had a list for every subject. If we asked him for a Reformation tract, he produced a list. If we asked him for 16th-century Central European politics, he produced a list. If we asked him for German economics, he produced a list. The lists were all poorly mimeographed but some of them offered treasures. Among the items that intrigued us was an early 18th-century economic study bearing the thought-provoking title: *Oesterreich über Alles.*

From one of the Nebehay brothers we acquired the great Rousseau discourse on inequality among men in first edition of 1755. And from the firm of Gilhofer we obtained, among numerous Luther sermons and Reformation tracts, a splendidly illustrated history of tournaments and jousts — Ruexner's *Thurnier-Buch* of 1566 that would go to our new friend "Molly" Pitcher of the Folger.

MS JOURNAL

This afternoon a dull meeting preceded by "Information from the President." In the American camp there is, we think, much cliqueing & considerable party politics. Not too interested in either.

We came to buy books — which we are doing — & to enjoy our-selves. So we sit on the fringe of the various cabals & observe.

To be chronological — the Heuriger, celebrating the new wine on Tuesday night was a riot. A handsome blonde Norwegian — Osbojrn Lungen Larsen — attached himself to me — discussed a painting entitled "The Scream," the works of Roald Dahl, & my wonderful eyes. He was quite something & me in a dither. The table abandoned me to him at frequent intervals — I left — he chased after me. Anyway, L & I finally scooted & took a tram back through the dark & empty streets of Alt Wien with heuriger on our palates & curious memories of the Scandinavian delegation. The next evening Fledermaus.

MS LETTER » **September 4**

The farewell banquet in Vienna Thursday night was held in Auersberg Palace — magnificent — decor, gardens, etc., though the food itself was nothing extraordinary & the speeches (14 — one for each country represented) were insufferable. Leona caused a minor crisis by informing the Directress of Seating Arrange-ments that she refused to sit where she had been placed — with the German delegation. An extra table had to be set up for L, myself, Lucien Gold-

M. and L. at National Bibliothek Prunksaal, Vienna, 1954

schmidt who just arrived, & another man. Quite a furor but L speaks her mind. We looked gorgeous in our evening dresses.

RETROSPECT The crisis that resulted from Leona's decision to make no peace with the Germans may have been minor but it had far-reach-ing repercussions. Winnie Myers would write a long letter to L justifi-

Place Cards at ILAB Banquet

ably claiming that if the Rostenberg firm was not sufficiently interna-tional-minded it should not attend an international conference. Leona could not help finding Winnie's indulgence about the Germans most illogical since she was such an ardent Zionist. In time their difference of opinion would be straightened out. Meanwhile, one of the members of the German delegation present at the farewell banquet was the dis-tinguished and highly respected Herr Domizlaff, who, seeing Leona, remarked to her, "Of course you will come to Munich and visit me." Her reply was as determined as her statement to the Directress of Seating Arrangements: "Of course I will not." And, to Domizlaff's per-plexed "Aber warum?" she replied with a vehement condemnation of antisemitic Germany and its entire population.

Since, as it turned out, Herr Domizlaff had been a warm and gen-erous friend of the Jews during the war years, we were both later abashed. Eventually we would visit him in Munich, and, after a frosty beginning, we would develop a good friendship with this erudite and fine man. As a matter of fact, he would one day give a supper party in our honor. But all that was far off in the future. Just now we had had a lesson in internationalism.

MS JOURNAL » September

From this Vienna in transition, what will emerge? The people must certainly be oppressed & humiliated by the revolving occupa-tion. Yet sacher torte, beer & heuriger still flourish — & imperial history is recited in a Vienna that is — what? Not imperial, not democratic — nothing but a center for subterfuge & political machinations in a sad time of occupation. Vienna has been quite an experience for us.

MS JOURNAL » **September 13**
We took the 8:12 from charming Kitzbühl [where we had vacationed] to Paris — a long journey enlivened for a while by an English couple in our compartment. They had brought their dog all the way from India and now are going back to London each in turn so the other can mind the dog who otherwise would be quarantined. . . . Had a $3.50 dinner — the worst of the trip — & were charged a Supplement of 500 francs each because from Basle to Paris the train went faster. We knew we were in France! Got to Paris about midnight — all smooth.

Unpacked this a.m. at the Scribe — & then to business. Visited some 5 dealers — bought about 40 from 3. Extremely interesting & very reasonable, bringing our average price down. Thiebaud is such a damned wily, cagey, shifty-looking Frenchman — a *Gaul* with reason. Said he had nothing for us — us being dealers — when we know even his W.C. is filled with books. Oh well, there are always more books in Paris. Did very well at Clavreuil & Magis. The latter had much early political stuff — our cup of tea. Wandered about the Left Bank all day — lunch at the Cafe Dupont — tea at our Salon de The on the Boul. Mich. . . .

LR LETTER » **September 15** » *10th Anniversary*
. . . Today was the 10th anniversary of L.R. LIVRES RARES. When I finally struggled to the breakfast table half awake, Mady presented me with an album entitled "Leona Rostenberg Rare Books. 1944-1954." The album is covered with enlarged photos taken by Cousin R. F. Koch, Esq., of our office (living room cabinets) with a red gilt-lettered spine. She had a table of contents & title-page printed & the album contains the entire pictorial history of the firm: e.g., announcement of opening Sept 15, 1944, original cable for the Pilgrim Press Calderwood, Mady's entry into the firm in April 1945, . . . covers of catalogues, letters of congratulation, trips to Europe,

clippings from AB, reviews of articles, letters & cards from notable customers, the rare books broadcast for MAC with Ben Grauer, etc. . . . I was almost comatose! In a state of complete elation, the firm purchased 2 tickets for "The Tales of Hoffman" at the Opera Comique ce soir.

LR LETTER & MS JOURNAL » September 15-16

. . . This afternoon was the grand jour in book buying. We visited a new firm (not new but new to us) — Chamonal on the rue Le Peletier. The place was mad with books, M. Chamonal who wears 2 pairs of glasses at once, & his assistant Gaston who collates as you buy. As we were popping up & down ladders, who enters but that sly, slick article, Jack Joseph of London, with cane, homburg, et al. Seeing us, he cried: "Ah, the beauties (ahem)." He immediately took over with a flow of execrable French — assured Chamonal he could trust us with his whole stock — the 2 beauties were très bien connues. Then he climbed a ladder holding his cane & homburg. Chamonal scratched his head & flew about in a flurry — a chubby, bright-eyed, rotund Frenchman who commands his assistant Gaston with a wave of the hand while he runs around, gesticulating & babbling away. The mad jabbering of French, the search for books, Joseph's muttering in English, M. Gaston's astonishment — it all required a camera. We bought 19 books from Chamonal including one absolutely superb item ($60) & added a picture to memory that is & must ever be unforgettable — a perfect afternoon in a Parisian bookshop. And it was fitting that we reached & passed our 400 mark on the Day of Days.

RETROSPECT The $60 "superb item" refers to the *Worstel-Konst*, a classic on the art of wrestling illustrated by the 17th-century Dutch artist Romein de Hooghe, who graphically depicted the grips, throws and tumbles. Years later we would find a second copy of that extraordinary work and exhibit it at the Book Fair in Tokyo at the time of the International Congress there in 1973. The firm of Isseido would find it irresistible.

As for Chamonal, he was the father of François Chamonal who would continue the firm, visiting us in America as we would visit him when he inherited his father's establishment. Today, after François' sudden death, his son Rodolphe continues the firm.

MS JOURNAL » **September 16**

We thought yesterday was red letter — but, as far as books are concerned, today was REDDER — in fact, the REDDEST so far. Today we bought 70 lovely, early, delicious books — a record for us.

We finally met M. Pierre Lambert of Chez Durtal in his boutique by appointment, at 10:30 a.m. We had been trying to reach him for 3 years, but he was always en vacance. Now he opened the shop expressly for us, & after our 44 purchases on the cash-&-carry plan, he assured us he will in future return from any vacance & open up for us. He is a Gallic version of Norman — silvery hair, thin, cravat, perfumed (all this is not a bit like Norman) but he is like Norman in his laissez-faire & indolent attitude about books, people & everything. His prices are most agreeably like Norman's also — & we had ourselves a feast plucking early, rare & interesting books & tracts from his dusty shelves.

The feast continued chez Andrieux on the Boulevard Malesherbes where another 26 brought the total of the day to 70 & the grand total to 499. I'll use red ink when we add the next and make it 500. The young proprietor has excellent & beautiful books, but we kept to those of a lower price range, disappointing him perhaps, but not ourselves. Nous sommes fatiguées, mais très, très contentes. Met Joseph again on the rue Jacob — ambling along the Left Bank with homburg & black umbrella like a stray cockney on the loose. Loud cheerios.

RETROSPECT We have written of the elusive Monsieur Lambert of Chez Durtal, who served as secretary of the Huysmans Society, in *Old & Rare*. Our plunder from his shelves in 1954 garnered for us — on the cash-&-carry plan — ephemeral pamphlets on French nobles, funeral orations on the Medici, a 16th-century treatise on the usefulness of reading history, a 17th-century attack upon Copernicus, descriptions of the Sainte-Chapelle and triumphal arches for the entry of a queen — books that illuminated the panorama of the past.

From the more staid establishment of Andrieux we found one or two fine highlights — the first edition of Pirckheimer's description of Germany containing early references to the continent of America, and a little French courtesy book for widows in which Pierre Dore in 1574 considered their plight and offered suggestions for their way of life. This last would go to "Molly" Pitcher of the Folger.

MS JOURNAL » **September 17**

We bouquined to the end. This a.m. to Picard, where we found just a few items amid the smell of cat pish in the theological rue Bonaparte, where the narrow sidewalk & the display of winged angels & crosses mingle with the odors of fish, meat, markets, & the above-mentioned distinguished scent. Then back to Clavreuil for a few more & in the afternoon to Sidney Baker, who lives quite far out — an Englishman deracine. He has lived abroad since 1914 — his wife is French. We found 4 little books, making our grand total the record number 508 — all fascinating, fine, lovely books. Capped the day with hot chocolate & noisette at Rumpelmeyer's (Angelina) & so it ends.

This has been the most varied of all the trips. London with its familiar streets & alleys, its gentlemen in homburgs & derbies, its Haunch of Venison Street, its kindnesses & courtesies, its flowers, its wretched weather. Vienna — the fascinating, strange city in transition between past & present — & the casuistries of the Congress. Paris — Left & Right Banks — old & delicious for exploring, magnificent & breathtaking for beauty — its old ladies in slippers & falling black cotton stockings, carrying their baskets of bread — its élan — crazy — ecstatic — impossible — all at once.

Mission well accomplished. We leave tomorrow at 8:16 a.m. for Le Havre — & the West. We carry with us food for thought as well as books & happy memories for the days that are to come.

1955

LR LETTER & MS JOURNAL » July 4

Crossed on the *Noordam* & docked at Rotterdam 6 a.m. Then to The Hague — Hotel des Indes. . . . As soon as we were settled in our luxurious quarters we went to Nijhoff on the Lange Voorhout, just down the street from us — one of the outstanding dealers here and at home. His stock is incredible. We asked for a certain elderly gentleman who had attended us in 1947 — Mr. Kern — he immediately recognized us and beamed benevolently — he is 77. By noon the firm had purchased 34 books and we are due to return this afternoon for further inspection. . . . We caught them just as they were preparing a law & political theory list & we snatched the early items from advance slips — a windfall for us. Of course it is raining & cold but we don't care. . . .

At Nijhoff a firm member asked us to meet a friend of his who wanted to dispose of family antiques. We did. He was Mr. Jelle Menage, who had helped 7 Jews to hide during the Occupation. He was betrayed, and in a concentration camp had to stand at attention from 4 a.m. to 9 p.m. naked. Now he has TB and must move to Majorca on a pension of $50 a month.

RETROSPECT The "snatch" at Nijhoff's included legal treatises on most phases of civilized life, from fiefs and dowries to salaries and privileges, from commercial transactions to criminal procedures, from feuds to libels, from war to peace. The Nijhoff cornucopia included a decree issued in 1568 by Philip II of Spain, curtailing a free press in the Low Countries, as well as a fine Russian edition of the edicts on crime and punishment promulgated by Catherine the Great.

MS JOURNAL » July 7

On the 5th we went to Meier Elte in the a.m. — nice art books, including an interesting Callot, & heard the stories of his hiding during the German Occupation — & his losses. We have shed more tears in Holland than anywhere else.

In the afternoon went to Amsterdam to see Hertzberger, but he had left to buy a library & his assistant took care of us.

RETROSPECT Meier Elte, now headed by son Max, was one of the leading continental art dealers. By 1955 this vivacious Hollander seemed to have recouped much of the loss he sustained in the war years, and we were able to buy from him several fine fête books as well as Callot's superb illustrations of the Siege of La Rochelle which we would sell to Mrs. John Nicholas Brown of Providence.

Menno Hertzberger was another survivor. Diminutive, dapper, enthusiastic, lively, he was known as THE LITTLE FATHER OF THE LEAGUE — a reference to his work in founding the International League of Antiquarian Booksellers. His English was impeccable and he was an unceasing source of amusing anecdotes and delicious stories. His taste was as impeccable as his English, and his shelves were filled with much that we longed for but could not afford. He would move from his impressive establishment on the Keizersgracht, the Internationaal Antiquariaat, to various other locations, ending in a small house in Blaricum, but wherever he was he was accompanied by great books. Through the years we would keep in touch; he would visit us in our country; we would schmoos long and often with him during the Congress in Tokyo in 1973. Like so many of the dealers who supplied us, he would become a warm friend. Meantime, in 1955, through the services of his assistant, we purchased from the Hertzberger firm a few early works including Martin Luther's great sermon on usury in a 1520 edition, and Philippe Galle's engraved *Imagines* of twelve Cardinals issued in 1598 and sold early in 1956 to our almost-associate Philip Hofer, head of the Department of Printing and Graphic Arts at Harvard.

MS LETTER » July 7

Yesterday a.m. we took the train to the little Dutch town of Hilversum & there visited a dealer (the business is carried on by the owner's widow) in a small, dilapidated palace with goat & dog outside. Mrs. Ludwig Rosenthal has one of the most immense . . . stocks of early books we've ever seen in one place — & we feasted on

Ludwig Rosenthal's, Hilversum, The Netherlands, July 1955

them. Went through stacks & stacks — rooms & rooms — & bought 55 of them!! All lovely — it was most successful. She drove us to her home for lunch, prepared by her housekeeper — very nice — & had also invited her assistant Miss Haas. All very pleasant — except for the sad tales we heard. We have done more vicarious sorrowing in Holland than anywhere else since the war. Mrs. Rosenthal gave birth to a baby in a concentration camp. The baby died, of course. She now has another child, Edith, age 7. Just last winter her husband died — in perfect health — 46 years old — died in 5 minutes from an injection for rheumatism — he was allergic to the stuff. She is a small, lugubrious woman dressed in black from head to toe — but she has BOOKS. Wonderful for us. . . .

RETROSPECT This was our first encounter with Hilde Rosenthal, whom we would visit annually for the next three decades. Like Hilde, who survived Dachau concentration camp and forged a new life in Holland, the Rosenthal firm of Munich, having been terminated by the Gestapo, was rebuilt in Hilversum. Much of the enormous original stock, which had been hidden and preserved by a loyal firm member, also survived, and now filled the shelves and stacks of that dilapidated "palace" outside which a goat grazed happily. To this stock Hilde Rosenthal would add with perception, knowledge and taste, and eventually her daughter Edith would follow in her footsteps. We too would follow Hilde, each year spending 2 or 3 days going through her descriptions while we consumed tea or coffee, socializing with her, enjoying her friendship, and with each visit adding great numbers of fine books to our stock.

On our first visit to her in 1955 our 55 purchases included a fascinating copy of a most significant work in Renaissance political theory, Hotman's *Franco-Gallia*. Bound with the treatise were a refutation of its principles and Hotman's brilliant replies to the refutation. Another important book in an unusual copy joined the pile of our acceptances. In her *Centones*, the 4th-century Latin poetess Falconia Proba had rearranged lines from Virgil to narrate the principal stories of the Bible. After Gutenberg's invention, her work would be called the first composition from a woman's pen to achieve the honor of print. We achieved the honor of purchasing it in a Venetian 1513 edition — a copy of extraordinary interest since it contained at the end a 14-page manuscript by a German Renaissance printer concerning Falconia's life and work. It was in an even earlier imprint — that of Strasbourg 1504 — that we acquired the collected writings of the distinguished Italian humanist Pico della Mirandola, a volume that bore an ownership inscription of 1505! Year after year, the promise of a visit to Hilde Rosenthal was fulfilled with good companionship, good food, and fine books. For the next few decades, the lure of Hilversum was not to be resisted.

MS JOURNAL, PARIS » July 9-10

. . . A few days in Paris. Yesterday picked last year's plummiest dealers — Chamonal, Andrieux, Lambert — but results were disappointing compared with 1954. Hope for better plums today. Books were not exciting. Met Davis at Chamonal's — he looked a bit taken aback. Will see him in London. . . .

Magis made up for the disappointment — had many interesting early law & political books. At Clavreuil bought a collection of 160 Mazarinades very cheap. A few nice books from Scheler. Knowing of our interest in political theory, he suggested we visit a dealer new to us named Michel Bernstein. Said we must make an advance appointment and he would arrange it since Monsieur Bernstein limits his customers! Scheler did phone and we are seeing Michel Bernstein tomorrow.

MS JOURNAL & LETTER / LR LETTER » July 12

Yesterday most interesting. Taxied out to see Michel Bernstein. He lives in a small turreted villa outside Paris, at Issy-les-Moulineaux, & has a lodge for his Negro doorkeeper & for his huge boxer Zouboulou. He sells only to the foreign market & has the largest & best stock of early political theory & economics, even surpassing Nijhoff. We spent 4 hours with him & could easily have spent another 4.

Bernstein seems to know everything. He knew L had worked for Reichner and told her that next to Goldschmidt she has the greatest knowledge of & reputation for the Renaissance period. He has been invited to speak at various American universities including Harvard, but can't get into the United States because of past political affilia-

tions. He was a member of the French Resistance & lived underground during the war.

When we first heard his prices — they rise, he instructed us,
from year to year — we told him in French that he should stay out
of business for 10 years & he would emerge a very rich man. He did
not think that was amusing — in fact, was insulted, but then, when
he said he knew Konigsberg very well and L told him her father came
from there, the ground was cleared, he softened, and we parted fast
friends. In fact he told us he would rearrange his vacation to be on
hand whenever we came.

We bought another collection of pamphlets from him and 37
books.

RETROSPECT Monsieur Bernstein's turreted villa had much in com-
mon, as it turned out, with Hilde Rosenthal's dilapidated palace. Both
housed great books in profusion, books directly in our fields of interest.
In 1955 we opened relations with them. Both would play a major role
in the development of our business as the years passed.

Of Michel Bernstein we have written copiously in *Old & Rare*: the
sound of his gummed soles creaking across the floor as he fetched a
book from its niche on a shelf; his instructions to us in his precise
French — "Ecoutez, mes amies"; his recollection of prices at a Salle
Drouot Sale; his lengthy commentary upon the French and the
American Revolutions — in that order.

Besides listening, we bought, and on that first visit we acquired several remarkable items from Monsieur Bernstein: *La Constitution de la
Lune* of 1793 by Cousin-Jacques, who envisioned a utopian lunar
empire where liberty, equality and the rights of man held sway; a French
treatise of 1588 on Mary of Scots who died for the faith at the hands of
English heretics; an extremely rare description of the Assembly
Chamber at Orleans used in 1560 for the meeting of the French States
General, its text accompanied by a large folding plate with full details
of the seating arrangements. We acquired also the book that broke the
ice between Monsieur Bernstein and us — the book that brought
Konigsberg into the conversation since it had been published there:
Kant's *Zum Ewigen Frieden* in first edition of 1795, the German philoso-
pher's hopes and plans for perpetual peace.

Despite our disappointment with a few former stand-bys, Paris — like Hilversum — had brought us fresh fields and pastures new. We would reap harvest from both as the years passed.

MS JOURNAL » **July 13**

After lunch to Leconte, Dorbon, & the elusive Librairie d'Argences & garnered a total of only 9 books. A pleasant evening with Emily D., beginning with dinner in a Basque cafe on the Blvd St. Germain & continuing with a bus ride to Neuilly, then back to the Place Kleber & a walk to the Etoile. The Arc illuminated — fountains playing on the Place de la Concorde — all so magnificent — & flags draped for Bastille Day all over Paris.

Emily Driscoll and L. in Tuileries Gardens, July 1955

MS JOURNAL, LONDON » **July 16**

Crossed over on the 14th . . . fog banks on the Channel delayed our little *Invicta* which stood still midstream. Arrived here after 8 p.m. . . . Saw McLeish yesterday a.m. — sweet — loquacious as ever — but got only 4 books. In the afternoon to Vellekoop. He now has 2 cats, & waxes languidly enthusiastic over his books. His assistant is *Lord* John Kerr, brother of the Marquess of Lothian, who fetched our books for us. Had tea & selected 16 books from the fiches & shelves — not enough, but maybe another day.

Had dinner with Nat Ladden last night — grand & scrumptious — at Simpson's — cocktails, roast beef, strawberries & cream. He treated & was very sweet. Much schmoos & a walk to Trafalgar Square & down Whitehall — buildings floodlit — & Nelson of Trafalgar Square faces Napoleon of the Place Vendome — both luminous but the former a bit taller than the latter.

We love it all so much!

M. and Nat Ladden, Hyde Park, July 1955

RETROSPECT Among the four books we bought from the loquacious Mr. McLeish were the *Memoirs of a Social Monster, or The History of Charles Price, . . . commonly called Old Patch*, the famous and infamous 18th-century English forger who would have so many followers; and, in first English edition, Contarini's *Commonwealth and Government of Venice* (London 1599) which Shakespeare used as a source for *Othello*. Nor had we wasted our time at Goldschmidt's either. From the languidly enthusiastic Jacques Vellekoop we obtained a life of the braggart captain Scaramouche that illuminated the Commedia dell' Arte, as well as a fine large set of Perrault's monumental *Hommes Illustres* copiously illustrated with handsome portraits of over 100 17th-century French illustrious.

MS JOURNAL & LR LETTER » July 17-20

. . . Yesterday a.m. to Gurney — not much — most of the miscellaneous shelves have been stormed by La Pitcher for Folger. Mrs. G. very pleasant — offered us iced grapefruit juice! Climate, it would seem, is the basis for the divergence of countries — not taste. The heat has got the English down — & they wear slacks & drink iced coffee. Wonders will never cease.

Afternoon — Weil — who muttered on about the extraordinary circumstances surrounding an edition that was a GEM because the author's mother-in-law printed her name in backwards. But actually, he's a darling, though his prices are terrible!! Had tea en famille — wonderful — cheese cake, strawberries & cream, homemade cookies — gorgeous. He is taking us to lunch, and he gave us a Roman coin of the Aldine Anchor that we'll have mounted here. We got a *Monde Dans La Lune* from him by Wilkins — 17th-century forecast of a lunar expedition!

To Thorp. He is still as shy as ever — left in the middle for Sotheby's & never said he was leaving or goodbye. The Thorp stock still includes many items collated by M.B.S. or L.R. & wanting a plate or a half-title. However, we found 10 books there including a Boyle on Colours with the chart — would have thrilled us a few years ago but we're getting blasé.

To Cecil Court & Seligman. His sammelband (the one we've declined since 1948, but examined & re-examined every year) is now £60 instead of £50 — serves us right. . . . But did get Aretino's comedies in the London John Wolfe edition of 1588. His "office" is so filled with books there's no place to stand — much less walk. I found myself clinging to the wall from the top of a ladder & trying to examine a book at the same time. Got several very nice items, however, and hope they're complete — including a Lomazzo *Pittura* of 1590 for £9/10/- ($26.60). Davis had said you can't find them anymore. On the whole, however, most English shelves are filled with insipidities, to wit: a complaint to the crown for the failure to stop a runaway horse; a sermon on the death of Mr. Andrew Horsefall; an ode to Queen Anne on the occasion of her sudden appearance in Kent.

M., *Ernest and Gertrude Weil,*
July 16, 1955

At Harding's no Mr. Wheeler & no books because they're all covered with cloth for the plasterers. At Grafton's no books because Miss Hamel has not bought any. Everything there still very "awkward" & Miss H. still hatted in last year's creation, sitting at her desk & looking around for enemies.

MS LETTER » July 20

. . . Spent the morning at one of London's highest priced dealers — Raphael King. We had never ventured there before, but did so this time & found him extremely garrulous. He knew all about us, & our "knowledge" & "hard work" & had discussed us the day before with Weil & Davis.

From the sublime to the ridiculous in the afternoon. Went to Norman's in Hampstead Heath. He & his shop have never been filthier. The place was inundated with debris — we stepped all over the books — while his son threw water all over the floor & tore pages from the books on the shelves. We picked up one little item encrusted with petrified dirt — but it was not a first of Grotius. In the middle, his wife asked FRAHNCIS to hold the baby, & he wanders about completely distracted & lost, runs out to see what his child is up to, & pays us absolutely no attention. He is really mad & his place will soon cave in with dung. The boy's toys are all over. A rag doll in the window. We stepped all over the books & managed to find 10 among the shambles. One of them may well be an extraordinary discovery. We have to work on it.

RETROSPECT Indeed we had made a find in the shambles of Hampstead Heath. And indeed we did have to work on it. The book we found was an anonymous French work actually by Louis de Montpersan, attacking the Jesuits, published in London in 1688. We bought it not for its contents but for a contemporary Latin inscription on the flyleaf that stated the work had come from the library of "the most illustrious and renowned Robert Boyle who had died in 1691." We felt that any book Boyle had owned would be one we would like to own.

When we started working on our copy of *La Politique des Jesuites* we learned that up to this point no book had been identified as having been part of the great scientist's library. Was it possible that, on the cluttered shelves of Francis Norman's wretched establishment, we had found the first?

Boyle's library, we learned, had not been sold at auction but rather "by Retail" or private agreement in July 1692, the agreement being that "Any gentleman or Others, may . . . Buy what they please at reasonable Rates." Apparently one gentleman present at the time had purchased Boyle's copy of a French work on the Jesuits that had, in the course of two and a half centuries, finally fallen into our hands.

It was entirely fitting that Robert Boyle, great scientist though he was, should have owned a work of religious interest. The author of the *Sceptical Chemist*, herald of modern science, had always had a deep interest in theology. Had he not been governor of the Corporation for the Spread of the Gospel in New England? Had he not written on the mutual service of science and religion? Had he not bequeathed funds for French Protestant refugees? This anonymous treatise against the Jesuits would have been precisely Mr. Boyle's cup of tea.

And so it had been. Once it had found a place on the shelves of Boyle's "small library" in Pall Mall. In 1692 it had passed to the anonymous "Gentleman" who had paid a "reasonable Rate" for it and inscribed it in Latin. Between then and 1955 it had doubtless passed through many hands until it achieved a different kind of anonymity by landing on Francis Norman's untidy shelves. Then, in 1955, it had passed to us. From us it would pass to the Yale Medical Library where it would be welcomed and cherished by Dr. John F. Fulton. It had come a long eventful way; it was freighted with history. Yes, we had made an extraordinary discovery that day in Hampstead Heath.

MS LETTER & JOURNAL » July 22

L made a splendid find yesterday. Here's the story: At a small dealer's — Burke's — in the outskirts of London, in an area smelling of bubble & squeak, she spied — on his travel shelves — *Austria As It Is*. It's really not a travel book at all, but an anonymous satire that was banned, & it has a fascinating history. Ever since we were alerted to it we've been hoping to find it. L grabbed it & only her unusual loquaciousness & pleasantries would have warned a dealer who knew her that something out of the ordinary had happened. It's a splendid copy, but Burke knew nothing about it & priced it at 10 bob — $1.40. It's worth at least $150, but the thrill of finding it is much more exciting than the money.

. . . This a.m. attended to L's research chore at Stationers' Hall & Somerset House, & in between ogled at the barristers in robes & wigs at the Inns of Court — not to mention the high-hatted, scarlet-frocked attendant at Somerset House.

This afternoon to Marks, where we got a few more — total entries now 418 — & where Plummer was, as ever, darling to us — letting us check prospective purchases in reference books, etc. Up & down stairs — up & down ladders. Exhausted.

Then to Joseph, who put on his vest & hat to escort us to his cellar — a few books only.

RETROSPECT A few years earlier, around 1952, we had driven to Ithaca, NY, to visit Felix Reichmann, head of rare books at Cornell. Reichmann had hailed from Vienna, effused Viennese charm, and was always a source of fascinating information. It was during our first meeting with him that he said, "If ever you find a copy of *Austria As It Is*, buy it for me. It was published anonymously in 1828, but it was actually written by an Austrian who fled the Teutonic system as I did and landed in America." We listened eagerly as Reichmann continued his narrative about Karl Anton Postl who had entered a monastery in Prague as a novice but had disappeared from there, fleeing for freedom from the Metternich autocracy to America. In 1823 he turned up in New Orleans under another name — Charles Sealsfield. He would live until 1864, and in the course of his checkered career he created a new type of fiction that would be labeled the ethnological novel. He himself would be labeled "Der Grosse Unbekannt" — "The Great Unknown." *Austria As It Is*, Reichmann explained, was no fiction. It was a violent denunciation of Austrian misrule, written in English and expressing the author's extreme liberalism and democratic convictions. Naturally its sale was strictly forbidden by the German and Austrian authorities, and the work was banned as libelous. Felix Reichmann craved a copy of the rare first edition. Now, thanks to Leona's find at Burke's in London, he would have it.

MS JOURNAL » July 25-26
Yesterday . . . bussed to the Tate. . . . saw the elongated agonies of the Pre-Raphaelites & the elongated elegancies of Sargent. . . . we sunned ourselves in Hyde Park, & read Orioli's *Memoirs*.
. . . Got 11 more very nice books at Dawson's (Feisy very affable in between jumping about) & Stevens & Brown (Ruth Collis sweet as usual — Brown mumbling affably away). Got a first of Pascal on Equilibre & hope it's complete.

RETROSPECT Two of the "very nice" books from Dawson's were Diderot's illustrated work on the blind — his *Lettre Sur Les Aveugles* of 1749 — and Priestley's *Experiments . . . on Different Kinds of Air*. As for the Pascal from Stevens & Brown — yes, it was complete.

MS JOURNAL » July 27
. . . Tomorrow we're off for Devon. Total score 459. Maybe more in Devon???

RETROSPECT By this time we had adopted the habit of combining a brief vacation with our European book hunt. As we had holidayed in 1954 at the Austrian resort of Kitzbühl, this year we decided upon a family hotel on Woolacombe Bay in Devon. The choice was not entirely fortunate since, during this unusually torrid summer, the coast was jammed with tents and caravans and the promenades swarmed with Britishers seeking relief from an unaccustomed heat spell. However, we could seek relief from the crowds in excursions to places where there were books. And we did.

MS JOURNAL » July 30 » *Woolacombe*
    . . . This afternoon took a long local bus ride to Westward Ho! to visit Miss Harper's bookstore. Despite our firm belief that no other American, however intrepid, had ventured there, we found that Miss "Molly" Pitcher had anticipated us. And so — bookless — we bussed back.

MS JOURNAL » August 2
    Spent today at Exeter. . . . Visited Commin in Cathedral Yard. He hardly spoke to us. We're tired of shy, eccentric, monosyllabic book dealers. We bought one book — curiously enough a first issue of *The Scarlet Letter* there in the shade of Exeter Cathedral. Maybe Hawthorne wouldn't have been surprised — but we were.

MS JOURNAL & LR LETTER » August
    Went to Salisbury . . . to the Old George Hotel which dates from the 14th century. Its rooms are oak paneled & its floors slope. In its courtyard (now a garden) Shakespeare is said to have played. . . . Went directly to Beach's where we found 3 books, much

M. at Exeter

chat, & L found her usual annual "wondrous" piece in England: an embroidered jeweled tinsel portrait of HENRY III in a handsome frame.

MS JOURNAL » **August 7**

Yesterday was filled to the brim. In the early a.m. to Stonehenge — unchanged after its 3,000 years in Salisbury Plain. Then to Wilton, estate of the Pembrokes, where Sidney wrote the Arcadia & the pre-Shakespearean theatre came alive under the genial auspices of his sister Mary — "Sidney's sister, Pembroke's mother." The park breathtakingly beautiful — great expanses of velvet green — a stone bridge over the River Nadder — giant, ancient Cedars of Lebanon — & an Italian garden whose classical statues have mellowed among the vivid flowers. Fine paintings within & Inigo Jones' architecture. We were taken into the private apartments too — saw the room occupied by the present Queen — in need of repair. . . .

In the library overlooking the garden, a tempting array of 17th-century calfbacks plus a double bed for the dogs. We were transported. A fitting climax to end the trip.

1956

August 4, 1956

SAILING TODAY

Transatlantic

NOORDAM (Holland-America). Rotterdam Aug.13: sails 11:59 p.m. from 5th St., Hoboken

MS LETTER » **August 14** » *The Hague*

. . . Had a fine crossing. . . . Landed Aug. 13 & saw Nijhoff that afternoon — interesting little items but not last year's windfall. Next day at Hilversum made up for it. . . . We bought more books than we have ever bought in a single day — 116 — from Frau Rosenthal. We took the 9 a.m. train & arrived there at 10:30. She had sent one of her "staff" to "fetch" us — & he took us to the converted mansion where she does business. She & Miss Haas were delighted to see us. With a short break for lunch at her home (lovely) we spent the whole day going over her books & slips. . . . Frau Rosenthal . . . was most attentive — plied us with tea morning & afternoon & a very good lunch. We sat down, ordering the staff about & generally taking over the whole establishment in our usual high-handed manner. We worked hard & worked them hard. Next day to Utrecht & bought well at Beijer's.

RETROSPECT Of those 116 books we selected from Frau Rosenthal's immense stock, one pointed the way we were about to go. Did we buy Poccianti's *Catalogvs Scriptorvm Florentinorvm* of 1589 because it was the first Florentine bibliography or because, for the first time, we were going to book hunt in Florence? Would we buy any of the 600 or more writings by such Florentines as Boccaccio, Ficino, Machiavelli, Varchi, whom Poccianti had included? If we did, we would have a bibliographical reference at hand.

MS JOURNAL » **August 26**

After much debate & inner speculation about the perils of flying, we flew from Amsterdam to Milan Aug. 16th via Frankfurt A/M. Just made the Milan-Venice train (not the Rapido).

How compress our 3 days in Venice in a word? I nearly fell into the Grand Canal when we arrived and walked across the station & found ourselves in this most completely unreal of cities. We took a gondola — with our 6 pieces of luggage — to the Danieli — & I shall never, never forget that night — gliding for the first time along the lagoon & the piccole canali — thinking each minute we would sink in the green waters — trying to express our fears in Italian — &

laughing so hysterically that there was water within as well as without the gondola.

And Venice — the Piazza San Marco — who can describe the bella ed immensa piazza con il famose campanile, il torre dell' orologio, la Basilica di San Marco, il Palazzo dei Godi. The mosaics of the Basilica — the 4 golden horses from the Arch of Nero — the wheeling pigeons — the great cafes where we sat in the evenings over a piccola bottiglia di Fiuggi. The gondola trip thru the canals — for 1,500 lire no explanations from the gondolier — for 2,000 he would talk. The walks in the back streets over the old, old bridges — the terra cotta casas & palazzi — the small canals. The day we went to Cassini's & found a few books. The afternoon we went to Murano, Burano, Torcello. The dinners on the roof of the Danieli overlooking the lagoon. The magical, unreal beauty of this incredible, unique city. The visit to the Accademia when we went on the crowded vaporetto. Like the mosaics of the Basilica, the days, the colors, the waters, the bridges, the domes, the turrets, the marble palaces sunk in the waters of the Adriatic — all take their precious places — another pictured tapestry that L & I have woven together.

RETROSPECT Trying to express our fears as we glided in our first gondola was ludicrously difficult despite the time we had spent the preceding winter studying Italian with one Signorina Snyder. Since the Signorina was intent upon teaching us conjugations rather than idioms, we found ourselves not only at a loss when we finally arrived in Italy, but tongue-tied. We never stopped trying, however, with often questionable results. Mostly, our Italian listeners would beg us to speak any other language but their own.

As for Signor Cassini, we found at his Libreria off of San Marco a work actually entitled *Libreria di San Marco* by its 18th-century curator Morelli. We could not have carried off from our Venetian ramblings a text more eminently appropriate.

MS JOURNAL » **August 26**

To Florence by air-conditioned Rapido last Sunday. . . . A week in Florence? A year is too little. Spent the first 2 days at Olschki's on the Via Vente Settembre. A delightful, dear man — & wonderful, wonderful books. He turned the whole place over to us (altho officially closed) — let us go through all his slips — & we bought 163 books at moderate prices. Invited us with his wife to Fiesole for dinner — bistecca fiorentina. . . . We spoke English, French, German, Italian (????) until Signora Olschki (a former contessa) begged us to converse in our native tongue. So much for Signorina Snyder! We got along famously.

RETROSPECT The great Olschki firm — no longer, alas, in existence — was part of the Rosenthal-Baer-Olschki cartel that for many years dominated the field of antiquarian books. Our visit in 1956 was to Cesare Olschki, a darling from first to last. From his amazing stock we selected books that reflected almost every aspect of the Italian Renaissance: orations on illustrious nobles, plays performed, art theory, the philosophy of divine love, the defense of women, civil life, letters from bloody battlefields. It was all there, interspersed with a few unexpected anomalies such as a novel entitled *The White Slave* purporting to be the autobiography of a Virginia slave, in which Richard Hildreth produced a forerunner of anti-slavery fiction. When those 163 Olschki books arrived they enriched our shelves with colorful accounts of Italian life, and they brought back to us our days with a great bookseller in his incomparable city.

MS JOURNAL & LR LETTERS » August 22, 24, 26
Visited a few other dealers here — but either closed or small pickings. Gonnelli — his shop with heavy stone walls & religious paintings hidden behind the Duomo. He spoke no English & hardly any French so we had to rely on our Italian which is quite execrable. Gozzini near by — mostly law books — and Signorina Cavalotti whose garbled English was about as bad as our spaghetti Italian. Found some Italian humanism, however.

. . . Always wandering thru the narrow streets with the dull yellow houses, green shutters, faded, ancient frescoes — a brief vista of the Tuscan hills — except from the Lungarno where we see the backgrounds of Renaissance paintings come alive before our eyes.

And what have we seen? The wondrous Fra Angelico frescoes in the courtyard & cells of San Marco, where Savonarola lived — the chapel frescoed by Giotto & showing Dante's portrait in the Bargello

— the superb, superb fresco by Gozzoli in the Ricardi Palace with Lorenzo the Magnificent on a white horse in the circling procession.

All for the glory of God — everything. The Pitti with its clutter of greatness from floorboard to ceiling — the Uffizi where greatness is better hung — *rooms* of Raphaels, Bronzinos, Titians, Del Sartos, some Michelangelo & Leonardo. Non c'e da dire veramente! It cannot be grasped at all.

And saw the studiola of Francesco de Medici in the Palazzo Vecchio on the Piazza della Signoria with its replica of David & sculptured clutter.

Florence has too much.

. . . And the churches that we run into at every other corner — Ognisanti — S. Trinita — S. Maria Novella where Margaret Fuller visited — the Masaccios & Ghirlandaios — fading on walls & ceilings for the glory of God & of Florence.

The shrines & niches — the coats of arms — the shadow of the Medici all over — the fortress of the Strozzi Palace.

An evening in the Piazza della Republica listening to songs by a fat Italian . . . who also played the accordion & moved a bow listlessly over a cello while she drank beer.

Santa Croce, with its tombs of Galileo & Michelangelo & Machiavelli. Casa Michelangelo. Doney's for tea. . . .

The awful pile of the Duomo — hideous mass of dull red & dull green & dull yellow. The doors of the Baptistry. Giotto's Campanile.

The clop, clop of the donkeys on their way to work every morning at 5.

The clop of the horses as we drive — 400 lire — the horses with their little white hoods.

The Ponte Vecchio with its shops — jewelry — leather — time & again we walked there.

This a.m. the English Cemetery in the heat — to worship briefly where Louisa Alcott worshiped — at the grave of Theodore Parker — but today no bird sang as if to break its heart. And Elizabeth Barrett Browning's grave — and Casa Guidi where the Brownings lived — right near the Pitti & the Boboli Gardens with their cypress walks, shaded grottoes & fountains, the amphitheatre & goldfish ponds. There we walked and recalled Cambiagi's 18th-century description of the Boboli Gardens that we had bought in London from Burke the year before and sold to the Met. Now it came alive for us and we breathed the essence of Florence.

This kaleidoscope of dull & faded colors — this medieval — Renaissance — Baroque city — borrowing only its noise from the present. Even tho we have seen it, we cannot quite believe it. But L knows the story of every stone & the tale told by this incredible city, where past is present & present scarcely exists at all.

Ah! Our weary feet — our dazzled eyes.

RETROSPECT We would return almost annually to Florence — for Florence and for books. Although we had always had 16th- and 17th-century Italian books on our shelves, our Tuscan sojourns would enrich not only ourselves but our business. Italy would never supplant France for us, but it would take a special place in our minds as well as in our catalogues. We would, as the years passed, issue several catalogues devoted to the Italian Renaissance, and we would also build up collections devoted to the Aldine Press and to the Medicis. Our first book hunt in Florence had been both seminal and productive.

LR LETTER & MS JOURNAL » August 28

Monday was for the books — entirely & literally. Left Florence by morning train for Milan, but broke the trip at a deserted, dirty, awful town called Reggio Emilia. Actually we had originally planned to stay there overnight, but Cesare Olschki rescued us from that experience. When he heard about our plans, he warned us not to bother staying there overnight. However, we had included it in our original itinerary and, as we shortly discovered, one member of L's family took this seriously and sent a letter addressed to LEONA ROSTENBERG at the Albergo Posta, Reggio Emilia! It turned out that the whole town knew about this. Anyway, we arrived at Reggio around 11:30 and were met at the station by one of the Prandi brothers of the antiquarian book firm Neroni & Prandi. We were never sure whether he was Dino or Paolo or Gastone, but we were well aware that he spoke nothing but Italian — not even Chinese, & that's what he sounded like. At any rate, we checked our luggage at the station & Signor Prandi took us to the Albergo to pick up L's letter & then drove us to the shop. The three Prandis hovered over us & pulled down books, gesticulating and explaining with fervor. At lunchtime — 12:30 — they closed the establishment & one of them escorted us to a so-called restaurant. As soon as he departed we did too, and tried to find a more attractive place. No dice. We landed in another dump where we ordered crackers, cheese and tea. The dirt & flies were free. Returned later to Prandi headquarters & completed our negotiations. Result: 34 books ranging from a 1537 legal treatise to an 1820 Bodoni catalogue — but mostly of course minor Italian humanism. Then on to Milan where we arrived around 7:30.

RETROSPECT WHAT PRICE BOOKS?

MS LETTER & JOURNAL » August 28
   . . . Milan a very exciting city — something like NY in its verve & vitality. Our air-conditioned room overlooks the Duomo. Arcades everywhere lined with gorgeous shops — floored in marble — frescoed ceilings.

   This a.m. went to the big dealer here — Hoepli. His assistant, or rather his Vice-Diretrice — an Italian Dottore, female, rotund, mustachioed — told us they had bought a big collection of early Italian plays — some very "hold" — from the 16th century. Would we like to see them? They were in the warehouse. Would we!

   Signora Dottore took us to the warehouse. And there we found our windfall. Row after row of neatly lined calf- & vellum-backs — a collection of 16th- & 17th-century Italian plays, all uncatalogued, all from the Landau Library — waiting for us. They will give us a price for the whole lot. You should have seen us in the warehouse. The Dottore was accompanied by *her* assistant Ferrante who pulled out chairs & ladders for us, bobbed up & down, bowed, etc. This was a wonderful stroke of luck for us. We're very excited & happy about it & hope to consummate the deal tomorrow.

RETROSPECT We did consummate the deal *domani*. Bought all the plays — 159 of them — for a little over $1,000. Our purchases thus far totaled 595 items, all of which we entered in a short-title list in a special ledger. These short-title entries were made on the spot — at the Maggs establishment in London while we sat at the Dickens table, now in Milan at a long wooden desk in the Hoepli warehouse. For our 1956 purchases we had to get an extra notebook, and there the plays from the Landau Library were listed on 29 August — first the 16th-century tragedies and comedies by Gelli or Speroni, Dolce or Trissino, Cecchi or Giraldi, from 1526 to the end of the century: plays with protagonists named Sophonisba or Hecuba, Medea or Giocasta, dramas concerned with Amor Costante or the Moti di Fortuna, La Pazzia or La Gelosia, La Moglie or Speranza. Then the dramas of the 17th century — plays that would go to Folger and Newberry, the British Museum and Toronto, Illinois and the collector Clifton Waller Barrett, in a cycle that had shifted from library to warehouse to library, with booksellers Rostenberg & Stern acting as puppeteers backstage.

MS JOURNAL & LETTER » August 29-30

We feel very much at home in Milan — its tempo like NY — very vibrant, & so different from medieval-Renaissance Florence, & the unique Venice. Our Italian is beginning to feel a trifle lubricated — wherever we go the firm is known with a "grand estime." After our Hoepli windfall we are combining some sightseeing with book hunting.

Yesterday afternoon to Signor Pozzi of Mediolanum — lovely books in cases reaching to the ceiling — high prices — but got 19 extremely interesting ones. Later took a horse & carriage to the Sforza Castle, actually an enormous fort dominated by a tower overlooking the city. This a.m. to Signor Vigevani of Il Polifilo — un jeune homme très serieux — but with prices that skyrocket. Got only 7. Dropped in to see Signor Cavallotti — nothing — but most kind & effusive & made an appointment for us with Rizzi tomorrow morning. Also visited Signora Marzoli, an effervescent Italian who loves America and was filthy from opening shop & never stopped talking the American lingo. Taxied out to Cenacolo to see *The Last Supper* of Leonardo — much better preserved than we had anticipated.

It has been quite a stay in Italy. Nearly 600 books plus Piazza San Marco in Venice, plus the Medici tombs of Florence, plus the Milan Duomo and Leonardo's *Last Supper*. Italy was graved in Browning's heart. For us it is graved in our minds and in our books.

RETROSPECT The Italian dealers for the most part were scholarly specialists. Signor Pozzi of Mediolanum, tall, serious, remote, but most courteous, was expert in the 16th century. From him we acquired, for example, Doni's treatise on art, his *Disegno* of 1549; a French pamphlet of 1589 on the meeting of the States-General at Blois; and a rare and fascinating poem by that celebrated Scot the "Admirable Crichton." This last was especially meaningful to us because Crichton's poem, extolling the glories of Venice, made an interesting link between Britain and Italy. We felt in 1956 that we as Americans had also made such a link.

At Il Polifilo we met one of the proprietors — Signor Vigevani, much younger than Signor Pozzi, equally serious, but a bit less unbending, and eager to talk about his family history which seems to have gone back to the time of Romeo and Juliet. Cavallotti we had first met at Irving Davis' — he always seemed to us extremely courteous, almost humble, but also slightly bewildered. He was probably more of a book scout than an established dealer.

Signor Rizzi, from whom we purchased a copy of a work on witchcraft by the Italian humanist Pico della Mirandola, was active in the Italian Antiquarian Booksellers Association, but he had an ingrained dislike of travel and refused to go anywhere outside of Milan. Unlike Rizzi, Signora Marzoli journeyed to the States periodically, always visiting great libraries and adding to their holdings. She was a good friend of Winifred Myers. If we were becoming Italianate Americans, Signora Marzoli filled the role of Americanized Italian.

Thanks in great measure to our Italian hunt, this had thus far been our best book-buying trip both quantitatively and qualitatively. At this point we hoped, as we wrote in a letter home, "to round out the purchases in Paris."

MS LETTER » **September 3** » *Paris*

. . . Spent the entire day at Bernstein's, the dealer in Issy-les-Moulineaux just outside Paris, & bought another *100* fascinating books. Total now 695 & we are ecstatic over our purchases — the best year yet for books. You will remember we met him first last year.

He & his wife were delightful. Had a very good lunch with them. They have a domestique from Guadeloupe & a boxer named Zouboulou, & all, including the dog, speak only French. So it was quite a day. He told us our last catalogue was a "chef d'oeuvre." His prices were moderate & he has the best collection of early political theory anywhere in the world. . . . He lives in an enormous house filled with books & is a most interesting person. They served aperitifs, wine with lunch & cognac after — so if I don't make sense, you'll know why. You can imagine we are tired — looking at his book slips (all of them), speaking French all day, etc.

RETROSPECT By this time we had learned much more about Michel Bernstein. His stock was indeed extraordinary — the result not only of his own intense interest in history and political theory, but of his scouring all of France — private estates, provincial abbeys, libraries suffering postwar casualties — for collections. In 1956 his shelves were lined mostly with 16th-century imprints on French government and its leaders: the Guise, Valois and Bourbon factions, and we feasted on them. One of them was a report of the St. Bartholomew Day Massacre and the assassination of Coligny in a Cracow imprint of 1573. Was not the future Henry III of France already King of Poland? — a fact that not only explained the Cracow imprint but gave the work a marvelous immediacy. To this we added Barnaud's violent protest against the Massacre in 1574, along with François Hotman's most notable work on political theory, his *Franco-Gallia*, in French translation. A 1580 treatise we selected foreshadowed the welfare systems of the 20th century. Entitled *La Police et Reiglement . . . des Pauvres de . . . Paris*, it discussed city hospitals, work of the city bailiff, and government administration for the poor of Paris. The *Police . . . des Pauvres* would go soon after our return to the Armed Forces Medical Library.

As the years passed, we would see the Bernstein imprints change to later dates — the emphasis on the 16th century would be replaced by concentration on the 17th, and that in turn by the 18th, notably the whole scope of the French Revolution and its aftermath. That metamorphosis did not reflect Bernstein's changing tastes so much as the increasing difficulty of obtaining early material on the subject.

MS JOURNAL » **September 5**

A full day. Galanti a disappointment but an experience. The floors are his bookcases, so it is almost impossible to bouquiner. Every few minutes he brings out from an anteroom a great monument, e.g., 1st of Rabelais. But he also has lesser stuff at higher prices. Tall, quite suave, & very peculiar. Got 3 books.

In the afternoon to Andrieux. Got 21 very interesting books & Mme. Vidal-Maigret gave us a very good discount. . . . L is deploring no find. I think we may have made a few without realizing it — & there is still time.

RETROSPECT The attractions of Baptiste Galanti had been touted to us by Irving Davis in London. Here in Paris Michel Bernstein had arranged an appointment for us. Accordingly we visited the rue Bazin and found ourselves in the helterskelter of M. Galanti's stock about which we have written in *Old & Rare*. Our purchases from that strange bookseller as well as the required manner of payment have all been recorded there: his books stacked from floor to ceiling in dizzying heights — but not on shelves; the iron chest concealed under his bed where moneys received were kept; his grandiose taste in books; his determined avoidance of "les taxes." He was, as we recall him after these many years, a bookseller against the grain whose personality was probably as peculiar as his business methods. But one visit was to prove enough for us. We never returned to the rue Bazin.

Even in the 1950s the fabulous, stalwart Mme. Vidal-Maigret was a mainstay of the firm of Andrieux. The house was devoted largely to conducting auctions in the Salle Drouot, but the overflow or underflow of unsold items found its way to Andrieux headquarters on the Boulevard Malesherbes. Year after year, for many years, we would make a point of returning there, always to be greeted affably, effusively by Mme. Vidal-Maigret with her exuberant, perhaps a bit perplexed comment to us: "Toujours fideles!" In those days it was easy to be faithful to Mme. Vidal-Maigret and the firm of Andrieux. It was there in 1956 that we found fascinating books from several centuries. A treatise of 1563 by Jean de Marconville on houses of worship among the Greeks, Romans and Hebrews was of both archeological and Judaic interest. The *Labyrinthe Royal de L'Hercvle Gavlois Triomphant* was an elaborate entree book of 1601 containing 14 plates depicting the triumphs and religious conversion of Henry IV of France. From Mme. Vidal-Maigret's shelves we also plucked 2 books on a subject of perennial appeal to us — women. One was *La Bibliotheqve des Dames* of 1640 by Grenailles; another, published 3 centuries later, was the *Bibliotheque* of one very special woman, the great French actress Sarah Bernhardt whose books were sold in Paris in 1923. We would sell the catalogue of her library to Harvard.

MS JOURNAL » **September 7**

What a day! Saw about 6 or 7 dealers & walked, walked, walked. Bought well from Chamonal. . . . 777 total now.

RETROSPECT Indeed we did buy well from Chamonal. One of the books we bought was Pierre Simon Fournier's celebrated *Manuel Typographique of 1764-1766*, a landmark in the history of typography. We paid Monsieur Chamonal "who wears his hat plus 2 pairs of glasses all the time" 18,000 francs net or $51.50 and sold it after our return to the Folger Shakespeare Library for $100. Several sets of the Fournier have passed through our hands, their prices climbing as their desirability increases. None is more desirable than the set we have in stock today, since that set came from the library of the great printer Robert Hoe III. For that set we paid at auction well over $6,000.

MS JOURNAL » **September 8**

Last day in Paris, & a beautiful one. . . . The sun is shining on the streets of Paris — on the Arc du Carrousel & the Arc de l'Etoile, on the narrow cobbled walks of the Left Bank & the grand vistas of the Right. Au revoir, Paris. Tomorrow London & the conference.

MS JOURNAL » **September 11**

Trip to London pleasant & uneventful — crossed Calais-Folkestone — arrived at the Cumberland about three-quarters of an hour late & had a mad scramble to change clothes, don our stoles & make an appearance at the welcoming reception in Park Lane. Everyone very agreeable — a crush — 250 people — all booksellers plus Pitcher.

RETROSPECT The opening reception heralded the 10th Annual Conference of the International League of Antiquarian Booksellers. We had attended a few of them — the one in New York of course, and the one in Vienna in 1954. There would be no political overtones here in

London with Peter Murray Hill as ILAB President. Instead there would be, we were sure, the unveiling of a London completely recovered from the post-war stresses and strains we had witnessed. Here too we were completely at home and we looked forward to this 10th Congress eagerly. So apparently did much of the book world — "250 people — all booksellers plus Pitcher." "Molly" Pitcher of the Folger was as usual persona very grata with the bookselling

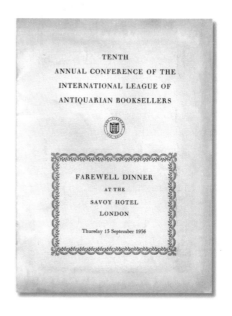

world. And in 1956, when antiquarian dealers were cooperating to build up not only their own trade but their relations with dealers all over the world, an attendance of 250 was not remarkable. Everyone, it seemed, wanted to participate in the development of our now international trade.

MS JOURNAL » **September 11, cont'd**

Yesterday a.m. to McLeish — still affable; to Grafton — still Dickensian but no longer amusing. In the afternoon the first conference — very dull — then to Goldschmidt. Went with Vellekoop to the cocktail party at Sotheby's. . . . Another mad crush. . . . This a.m. to the elfin Mr. Davis & total is now 807 — beyond our dreams. Got one lovely architectural book from him, the rest minor.

RETROSPECT McLeish was not only still affable but still a good source. One of the books we bought from him in 1956 was *The Tryal of Nathanael Thompson* issued in London in 1682. That find was particularly timely to Leona. Just the previous September, the British bibliographical journal, *The Library*, had published her article entitled "Nathaniel Thompson, Catholic Printer and Publisher of the Restoration." In it Leona had elaborated on the career of the printer-publisher who had been tried and condemned for circulating books of

Catholic interest. That article would become a chapter in Leona's two-volume history of 17th-century printing. Meanwhile, we sold our copy of the Thompson *Tryal* to a far-off university in the British Commonwealth of nations, the University of Sydney!

As for Vellekoop, before going off to the Sotheby cocktail party with him, we took from his shelves an early edition of Erasmus' plea for universal peace, the *Querela Pacis*, as well as a 1519 eulogy of the Holy Roman Emperor Maximilian I. The latter is of interest because its history reveals the strange ways of the bookselling fraternity. We bought it from the firm of E. P. Goldschmidt in 1956 and 3 years later sold it back to that firm for a small profit. The architectural book we found at Irving Davis' was a French study of architectural terms published in 1572 which we would sell to the Avery Architectural Library of our alma mater, Columbia University.

MS LETTER » **September 12**

Yesterday a highlight of the Congress. Put on our summer evening dresses & stoles (woollen underwear underneath) for Covent Garden, where we were treated to the most beautiful ballet done by the Sadler's Wells group — Swan Lake — simply wonderful. After that we had a champagne supper for the booksellers right in the theatre. Delicious food — smoked salmon, chicken, ham, roast beef, shrimps, cakes, ice cream, fruit — & oodles of champagne. We had a lovely table graced by the two handsomest men here — Jacques Vellekoop & my old Norwegian friend from Vienna days. All very gay & everybody very friendly. It lasted till midnight. Marguerite Cohn of House of Books gave us a lift back to the hotel and told us to call her "Margie." "Everybody who likes me calls me Margie."

MS JOURNAL » **September 13**

Yesterday the excursion to Greenwich — a boatload of booksellers in search of the meridian line — lunch on the lawn — a sunny, pleasant day. Returned to town with Hilde Rosenthal and Jacques Vellekoop.

This a.m. to Maggs & got some stuff that interested us more than it did Clifford — a 1573 Vilna imprint about German illustrious, a 1591 Lomazzo on the Muses, and a rare mid-16th-century Italian report of the absolution of England by the Pope through the efforts of Cardinal Pole.

Total now 821 & our well — our bank account, that is — all but dry.

Next international meeting will be in Munich & we'll be in absentia. Tonight the banquet to end this 10th annual Congress. Hope L & I will be at the same table.

MS JOURNAL & LETTER » September 14

We were at the same table. The farewell banquet was really most elegant. It was held in the grand ballroom of the Savoy Hotel — handsome decor, crystal chandeliers, a major domo in red jacket who announced us as we entered & cried out, "DINNAH IS SERVED" & "PRAY SILENCE FOR YOUR LOYAL TOAST" (To The Queen). The President of the English Chapter — the actor-bookseller Peter Murray Hill — wore his insignia — looked like the Order of the Garter — & everyone was in full evening dress. Really a magnificent spectacle that put our international banquet to shame. The dinner was superb — all kinds of wine & liqueurs — a sherry turtle soup, sole, filet mignon in madeira sauce with mushrooms, & the dessert a marvelous Baked Alaska with cherries & little cakes. Speeches long, but not too bad, & later they had a cabaret, dancing, & a late buffet. There were 380 people there. . . . each lady got a beautiful souvenir at the banquet — a real Wedgwood ash tray. We are light years away from post-war austerity now.

MS JOURNAL & LETTER » September 14-15

In the afternoon to the erratic & impossible Norman whose dungheap still yields treasures given away & tea at Dr. Weil's. Our total — grand & official — is now 849 (really more because there are extras bound with). The best trip ever — the zenith — for book buying. And the trip, now all but over, perhaps the best ever. We're packed, ticketed, labeled. Tomorrow a little more prowling — & then the 5:03 boat train — & Westward Ho again. Goodnight, my diary of 1956. Sweet dreams of all that's passed.

1957

MS JOURNAL & LETTER » August 5-6, 10

We started off with a bang — 48 books plus 55 tracts, mostly 17th-century stuff & very interesting. As soon as we got to The Hague we sallied forth immediately to Nijhoff's where Mr. Kern greeted us like long-lost friends, and where we bought not only books but a collection of Flemish pamphlets.

That afternoon to Elte, one of the Dutch dealers whose books the Nazis stole during the war. He's reassembled a fine stock & we tea-ed & booked with him.

Next day spent at Hilversum. Mrs. Rosenthal on vacation — spent the day with the energetic Miss Haas & had lunch with her at the Palace Hotel, a very decorous, pretty, & quiet place for retired & retiring elderly ladies. She is going to drive to Switzerland in her scooter (like a motorcycle) for her vacation, although she must be damn near 60! Books better than last year — extremely interesting & we were well pleased. Our Dutch stay has garnered us 162 books plus the placcarts.

Wandered about The Hague — canals where old men and boys fish and ducks & swans swim — leafy alleys — cobbled streets — the "Passage" like a miniature "Galleria" where we bought some stamps — smell of flowers in the air — & sunshine for a change, all over.

RETROSPECT The pamphlets we bought from Nijhoff consisted of 55 royal edicts relating to Flemish political, foreign and domestic affairs from 1597 to 1636 — all bound together in vellum. Our growing passion for on the spot political ephemera had extended now from France to other countries. Just as our French pamphlets reflected the life and concerns of their time and place, so the Flemish mirrored their particular mores. Such material, designed as throwaways, had — to us — become keys to the past.

The books we selected from the Rosenthal shelves reflected the astounding variety of her holdings. There was, for example, a life of Tamerlane the Great published in 1553 that might have been the source for Christopher Marlowe's *Tamburlaine*. There was a 1529 German translation of *The Supplication of the Beggars* by the English pamphleteer Simon Fish that was one of the earliest relations of poverty in England. And, across the world and across the centuries, there was *The*

North Georgia Gazette, a weekly journal edited in 1821 by Sir Edward Sabine during his stay at Winter Harbor when he was searching for a Northwest passage. The shelves of Hilversum seemed to encompass the whole world.

MS JOURNAL » **August**

Came here to Brussels. . . . We put on our rain togs & taxied to Moorthamers. At first thought there'd be nothing but after much digging did find about 20 very interesting books. . . .

August 9 we taxied to the "Gallerie du Commerce" — like Cecil Court — only no old books — then dropped in at Castaigne where a young man brought up books one at a time from the "cave" — then Miette — so expensive. At 2 kept our appointment with Van der Perre — white-haired, crusty geezer — with loads of books — but most of them in wooden crates. . . . Then on to his daughter Francine van der Perre — as affable & charming as he is forbidding — but no books. . . .

August 11

Yesterday a.m. . . . visited several minor dealers in Brussels — Deny almost on top of the Mannekin Pis — Van Loock, Le Clercq . . . got a few books. After lunch to Liege — Gothier practically under the Cathedral. A huge warehouse of a place with narrow circular stairs & books in stacks "protected" by a wobbly railing where we crawled around in fear & trembling. Belgian total nearly 90 but hard digging for them.

Dashed into the Cathedral . . . & had dinner in the Metropole Grill — quite a place. There is a stream of visitors to the toilettes while the band plays & the chanteurs chantent & people in pot-like hats greet each other with a triple kiss. Very gay & lively — we spent most of the evening there watching Brussels en fête de samedi soir.

RETROSPECT This was our first and, as it turned out, our last visit to Belgium in search of books. We sandwiched it between Holland and Switzerland, and although we scouted more than half a dozen different stocks, we seem to have omitted what might have been a major source of supply. Intimidated by his reputation for very high prices, we never ventured to the establishment of Florian Tulkens. Years later, at the time of the ILAB Congress in California in 1967, we would meet M. Tulkens and enjoy our acquaintance with him. As a matter of fact, 30,000 feet up in the air, when we were all en route from New York to the West Coast, we would sell him a book we were planning to exhibit at the California Book Fair, one of the earliest biographies of that feminist visionary Joan of Arc.

As of the moment, in Brussels and Liege, we had gathered together a number of bread-and-butter books. A few, however, were spread with jam: a Hotman of 1588 on the rights of the Bourbons that we found at Deny's and sold to the Newberry Library; and several interesting treatises that we acquired from that "crusty geezer" Van der Perre — a Beze of 1576 on the jurisdiction of magistrates; the great work on a democratic government by Languet, his *Vindiciae contra Tyrannos*; as well as 2 rare French expressions of concern issued in 1649 at the execution of Charles I of England. What we would have added to our Belgian bundle had we visited Tulkens must remain conjectural.

MS JOURNAL » August 12-13

Took the Trans-Europe Express at 2 — best train we've ever been in in Europe — with a stewardess as on airplanes. Passed Namur — Luxembourg — Strasbourg (sighs for the snows of yesteryear) — & here — Basle — at 8.

Basle is dear, sweet, neat & charming but has NO BOOKS. Found only 14 at Haus der Bücher this a.m. Seebass & Frau Thamann very charming — but in OLD & RARE they have MIDDLE-AGED & OVER-

Haus der Bücher (Erasmushaus), Basle, 1957

DONE. Worse still, all the so-called antiquarian dealers listed in the Directory are either out of existence, dead, or have nothing but modern books.

We walked & walked through the "gasses" & "strasses," saw Wepf & numerous others, but nothing at all. Very disappointing. Will meet the Bibliothecaire en Chef of the University Library tomorrow & hope for duplicates. . . . The town is old, very, very neat, as if designed by a meticulous draftsman with very clean fingers. The Rhine divides it, & it has little parks with flower borders. But it has NO BOOKS! . . .

This a.m. (August 13) spent at the University Library — found 6 — offered $25 — OK. Dark & cold there — lights turned on for only a few minutes — all the traditional economies of Europe despite the fact that this is the richest of its countries. But for $25 they sure gave us an awful lot of their time.

Then Seebass & Frau Thamann took us for a full-course dinner including wine that lasted 2 1/2 hours — schmoosed re books & booksellers: "What's with Nebehay?" — "What's with Hertzberger?" etc.

We would like 3 hours in Basle in the year 1520 to observe, and to collect books cum autographs. . . .

RETROSPECT Despite our low estimate of the books we found in Basle in 1957, we wish we had every one of them back today! We'd especially like to have the treatises by the mid-16th-century Italian reformer Curio that we bought from the University of Basle and sold to Folger; or the Venetian Academy imprints of the Aldine Press; or the early Luthers that came from Haus der Bücher. The passing years have added to their rarity and wrought a sea change.

MS JOURNAL » August 16-17

Zurich is a most beautiful city — the hotels cluster round the lake which is dotted with white sails & regal swans, & surrounding it are snowcapped mountains. There are only 2 troubles with this flourishing magnificence — lack of sun & lack of books.

Yesterday a.m. we visited Frauendorfer at L'Art Ancien but got only 12 books — a great disappointment. Frauendorfer advised us to book hunt in Geneva. We visited most of the Zurich dealers — with meagre results.

How they can list themselves as antiquarians when they have so little printed before 1900 is a conundrum & a provoking one. We bought a bit here & there — from Schumann & Laube.

Spent the whole day today at Berne. Saw most of the dealers & found 20 good books among Voirol, Lang — an industrious young man, très sérieux — Alder, who is the Swiss equivalent of Norman even down to the smell of his place — & Hegenauer.

Back in Zurich stopped at Madliger & got 8 unexpected very interesting books.

RETROSPECT   One of the more attractive items we found at Voirol's was the *Histoire Secrette* of a most attractive lady, the Duchess of Portsmouth, mistress of Charles II of England. It had been published in 1690 by Baldwin, one of Leona's stable of 17th-century English printer-publisher-stationers. The BSA had published her article on his firm; now this imprint of his would go to Folger.

The books we purchased from the other Berne dealers presented studies in contrast to the free and easy Duchess, being for the most part works about very staid pedants and very single-minded reformers.

MS LETTER & JOURNAL » August 20-21

Ensconced in the Hotel Metropole, Geneva, facing Lac Leman, the fountain & the geyser. Since yesterday we have visited 4 dealers & bought 66 fine books — about as many as we got in Basle & Zurich combined. Bader (whom we had telephoned from Zurich) came in from his country place at Nyon to open his shop for us. A delightful man who likes to go fishing, but who sold us some of his splendid books anyway. He took us out for an aperitif & showed us all around the old part of the city where most of the booksellers are. Then he took us to another dealer — Burstein — from whom we got 16 books. We are having tea with him again on Friday.

Saw Slatkine & have an appointment Friday a.m. with the latter's brother who is said to have a fine 17th-century collection. Here's hoping!

Geneva has great élan & is like a miniature Paris — the old city with its mementoes of Calvin so reminiscent of the Left Bank, & the modern city on the lake front. Not so lieblich as Zurich, but vital & exciting. From here we'll make excursions to Chamonix & Lyons for plaisir & books. . . .   We have never been in French Switzerland before & it is most fascinating to us.

RETROSPECT   From Bader we got much charm and chocolate, delicious gateaux and delicious memories, but it was from the brothers Slatkine that we acquired a few truly provocative books. One of them was La Harpe's revolutionary analysis of French Revolutionary language, his *Du Fanatisme Dans La Langue Revolutionnaire* of 1797 in which he foreshadows William Safire in his comments on language. According to La Harpe, "One is forced today to use these new expressions to describe the enormity of the crimes committed." Another Slatkine trophy was Mallarmé's prose translation of the poems of Edgar Allan Poe with illustrations by the great French impressionist Edouard Manet — a truly compelling association of names.

MS JOURNAL » **August 23**

A perfect day yesterday — Montreux. Passed through Vevey & thought of Louisa May Alcott who met "Laurie" there before putting him in *Little Women*. And the Castle of Chillon. Can't help thinking what a romantic thriller a life of Bonivard would make — the fortress overlooking the lake — dungeons, rats, turrets & round towers, gothic arches — & the Duke of Savoy living above in 16th-century elegance. The views so wonderful — vast expanse of Lake Leman, glistening in the sunshine & the mountains surrounding it. Ambled around Montreux, lunched in one cafe along the lake front & tea-ed in another — window-shopped — & reread Byron in the gen-u-ine setting. A day for the books — a happy one.

MS JOURNAL » **August 26**

This a.m. to Rauch — the Rosenbach of Geneva — bought 3 books including a Dutch Grapheus for $85. By this time all the dealers seem to have heard about these 2 Americans who are the busiest gals in Geneva, and they ask, "You are still here? When are you leaving?" They must think we're after buried treasure. Ambled on in the vieux cité, and there Sack apparently recognized us and invited us to "amuse ourselves" inspecting his "cave" — "depot" — warehouse, & sent an old geezer along to light it up for us. It was a dungeon with cobbled floors & great wooden doors and we found a few nice little bread-&-butter books.

MS JOURNAL » **August 28**

Yesterday one of the really memorable days & if I begin to sound like the MS of 1925 on her first trip abroad en famille, I have reason. We bussed to Chamonix. In the bus the usual assortment of tourists — 2 NY schoolteachers, behind us two Italian ladies, & in front another American teacher. These kept up an antiphonal obbligato of chatter the whole way there & back. At Chamonix, took 2 cable cars till we reached the Brevent — 8,500 feet high — swung across an immense gorge. Howling winds. A hail storm. Vast panorama of the snowcapped Mont Blanc massif — glaciers — a mountain lake. We were far above the timber line & I was scared unto death — could hardly move from cold & fear — & I have a hearty respect for mountains. Too bad we had no sun, but in a way the mountains seemed more awesome in this desolation. I have never seen anything at once so grand & so terrifying, for the Grand Canyon, to me at least, was not terrifying. Came down again from the tops of giant pines to their feet in tier after tier of the descent.

It rained in Chamonix, & we gorged French pastry, wandered about the knick-knackeries & ended up huddled in the station. Freezing cold despite vyellas, sweaters, woollies, suits, coats, wool socks. Bussed home along the great mountain ranges, waterfalls, chalets, farms — to the tune of that unending antiphonal obbligato — Italian in the rear & American history in the front — not to mention an English boy who took sick & had to have the car stopped. But despite the hazards of bus excursions, this was truly a day to remember — a WONDROUS one.

Tomorrow at 12:30 we leave for Milan and our 10-day Genevan stay is all but ended. A delightful interval to remember — the narrow streets, winding upward, in the Vieux Cité with its "Antiquites" "Librairies" — the lakeside & the quais with their tooting paddle steamers — the stores on the rue du Rive — the rue du Rhone — the sparkling waters of Lake Leman — the Jet d'Eau shooting upwards & catching a rainbow — and especially the booksellers who kept wondering why we stayed on. L bought me a wood carving of a monk with a book whom we have christened John Knox. Even Calvin would be pleased. And I am happy with this memento of our Genevan passage.

MS JOURNAL & LETTERS » **August 30-September 3** *Milan*
We arrived in this European version of New York on Thursday & were immediately ensconced in our old stream-lined hotel — our

window facing the Duomo, from which we could easily pluck a saint or a gargoyle. . . .

We are here — back to the elaborately sculptured Duomo, the bustling Galleria with its animated tin soldiers, the Castello Sforzesca, the crowds, the ancient churches tucked away behind modern office buildings — & we have already bought well. 52 books — the majority from the very good dealer Pozzi who has a vast & extremely interesting stock.

For the first time went to the Libreria Vinciana — an enormous stock of Italian books — & we are in the midst of choosing. We return there in the afternoon after siesta (one must "see Esther" in spite of the fact that it is very cool & overcast). Continued the hunt after siesta & found more little political theory books very cheap.

At the Libreria Aldo Manuzio we caused a crise Italienne. When I wanted a ladder I asked for an elevator in my unspeakable Italian, & when I wanted a chair I asked for a church. Since the padrone spoke only Italian & was a timorous soul to begin with, he was completely overwhelmed by us & we were struck dumb in Italian. When L finally offered him a traveler's cheque, he refused, & trembled with fear & excitement.

On to the famous Hoepli warehouse where their aide-de-camp Ferrante met us & demonstrated very "hold" books — mostly 19th-century leftovers from libraries, with prices to be supplied "domani." Then to the elegant . . . Signor Chiesa who is quite a snob about books, but we found a collection of Porzio & a 17th-century book on the dowsing rod.

Saw another small dealer — Sgattoni — & found a few books — then back to Hoepli where we "adjusted" prices of the warehouse books & went upstairs to find more. Eschlimann & Radaeli most cordial despite our "small" purchases.

Tomorrow our last day in Milan — we leave for Paris by the night train.

RETROSPECT Although we did not buy any collection of very "hold" plays from Hoepli this year, we did find at Signor Pozzi's Libreria Mediolanum some early feminism in the form of a 1526 defense of women by the Italian historian Capella and a 1562 Protestation by Elizabeth of England calling for peace and order within her kingdom.

More important than any single Milan purchase was our introduction to the firm of Vinciana operated by the charming Dottore Sandro Piantanida. For many years we would return annually to his shop, spending hours plucking from the Vinciana shelves those 16th- and 17th-century Italian commentaries and studies that restored the background and reanimated the protagonists of a bygone world. From Signor Piantanida we bought instructions on civil life or family government, eulogies of noble Venetians, treatises on the master of the household or the leader of a nation. From the birth of princes to the death of kings, from the demands of war to the needs of peace, here was a panorama of another age. Here were those "Frutti della Historia" that we labored to learn. Signor Piantanida was well aware of all this. Eventually he would issue a four-volume catalogue of his 17th-century holdings that would encompass the age. Meanwhile, year after year we would return to his doorstep, linger over his offerings, and even, on one glorious occasion, raid his cellar for collections set aside. The fruits of Signor Piantanida would indeed be the fruits of history for us. We savored them first in 1957.

MS JOURNAL » **September 4** » *Paris*

How happy we are to be back in Europe's first city. We feel so at home — love to look once more at the beauty of those vast expanses — Arc de Triomphe du Louvre — Place de la Concorde — Arc de l'Etoile — & the familiar, dear Left Bank — Notre Dame's two shoulders rising out of the Seine — or so it seems when one crosses the Pont du Carrousel.

. . . We left Milan for the train — the Simplon Orient Express that had come from Athens and Istanbul! Quite comfortable if a bit cramped, & fortified with sleeping pills we both slept despite the rough road bed.

. . . I'm so happy to be back in my French. And here we are together in Paris, which is becoming as beloved as London, tho far more beautiful. Tomorrow Bernstein — then we shall see.

MS JOURNAL » **September 6**

Too exhausted to do more than record the high spots —
Yesterday a.m. to Chamonal, where we saw M. Gaston & Chamonal
Fils. . . . Got 27 very nice books. Took the metro to Issy after lunch
& got to Bernstein's at 2. Did not leave till 8 — the whole time going
through his fiches & plaquettes. Got 101.

Bernstein told us that during the war 2 dealers circulated a peti-
tion to prohibit Jews & foreigners from selling books in Paris — &
80% of the Paris dealers signed it! We also heard that about 20 French
dealers are going to Munich for the Congress. Bernstein gave L
counterfeit stamps he & his wife had printed while they were in the
Underground.

Between bouquinering & schmoosing in French all day with M.
& Mme. B., we were completely done in by the time we got back to
the Scribe — had dinner & went to bed. Such a day!

RETROSPECT Chamonal Pere was giving way to Chamonal Fils. We had
merely caught glimpses, so to speak, of the Pere — he was apparently
headed for retirement by the time he entered our ken. Naturally we
would become closer to his son François. When we first met Fils he was
a jolly, rotund young man who savored his books, his profession, and les
bons vins français. His enthusiasms were contagious. We would visit him
many years annually, on the rue Le Peletier, lunch with him from time
to time, and eventually be introduced to his son Rodolphe. After François'
untimely death, his heir apparent Rodolphe would succeed to the
Chamonal throne. Now, in 1957, among the "27 very nice books" we
acquired from Chamonal were a description of the Strasbourg Cathedral
that carried Leona back to her student days, and another copy of that wonderful Utopian bundle that included in one volume Hall's *Mundus Alter
et Idem*, Campanella's *City of the Sun*, and Bacon's *New Atlantis*.

Of course a lengthy visit to Issy exhausted us. Like most
Frenchmen, Michel Bernstein believed that his language was superior
to any other, and like many Frenchmen he had a provincial attitude
toward anything that was not French. Although he may well have
understood and read the English tongue, he never spoke it. Both his
travels and his discourse were confined to the borders of France. As a
result, while we certainly polished up our French during our long hours
at Issy, we also were thoroughly wearied at day's end.

Already in 1957 Bernstein's stock had begun its climb to the 18th century. While we still found among his fiches a number of 16th- and 17th-century imprints, we were beginning, under his powerful influence, to move up to the 18th century and its Gallic climax in the French Revolution. It is true that we found at Bernstein's a beautiful collection of 37 French pamphlets all issued in 1589, concerned mostly with the trials and tribulations of Henry Valois. But we also found several intriguing pamphlets issued at the time of the French Revolution. To us perhaps the most interesting were those French Revolutionary imprints that were concerned with affairs across the seas in our own country. We added to our Bernstein prizes, for example, Fauchet's *Eloge* of Franklin, as well as a *Lettre D'Un Americain aux Citoyens Francois, Sur La Representation* in which the French citizenry were informed of the glories of American rights and liberties. Our mania for France already had a side effect in our growing passion for Franco-Americana. Both were passions that Michel Bernstein could satisfy.

MS JOURNAL » **September 6-10**
 . . . This a.m. to Jammes (some very sweet early French novels). . . . Exhausted . . . don't even know what we did today — but we adored it. Got to 2 dealers — Clavreuil, who was at the chasse which is sacred to him, & Magis — only 10 books all told. We get fussier every day — which is healthy.
 . . . La pluie tombe sur les toits de Paris & it has been falling all this Sunday. But we did not care. We had a lovely, happy day anyway. Around noon dashed to the Stamp Fair on the Rond Point off the Champs-Elysées — wonderful — lots of fun — found stamps we wanted, & if it hadn't been so rainy would have found more. Anyway it's an exciting way to get stamps, going from stall to stall. Paris thinks of everything!
 . . . Kept our 4:30 appointment with Lambert. He is still very active in the Huysmans Society, still very precieux, literary, Catholic, reactionary, & enjoys poor health. An interesting little man, but he does not seem to have changed his stock in 2 years. Found only 7. We are *very* fussy.
 Then walked along the bookstalls on a busman's holiday to Angelina's for hot chocolate & pastry, without which no Paris stay

would be complete. Deliciously full of whipped cream, we walked through the narrow streets back of the rue de Rivoli in the rain to the Scribe — & here we are, happy after our rainy Sunday in Paris. It isn't raining rain, you know — it's raining whipped cream.

. . . To Dorbon, where the marked prices were not "good," and had to be raised but could not be revealed!! Then Petitot who wrangled about the discount but gave in when we paid him on the spot. He had some nice books including a handsome entrée which is now ours. . . .

And so it ends again — our last day of bouquinering — or buc- caneering — on the Left Bank. This afternoon to Andrieux. Total is 765 not including plaquettes or bound-withs. Since we found no big collection anywhere, & since good books are becoming scarcer every year, & since we have only $350 left of our allotment — we are pleased with ourselves. Another good trip. And here's to the next.

RETROSPECT By 1957 we had more or less established the cast of book- selling characters who would continue to supply us with books. The French variety bore many points of contrast with the British. There were many more French antiquarians to begin with, but their stocks were considerably smaller. In addition, they were, we thought, more precise about their books, usually taking more pains to collate them and describe their condition. On the other hand, they were often less friendly, far less outgoing, far more suspicious of foreign intruders from overseas than the welcoming antiquarians of England, for example. One could not establish rapport with them in one session — any warm rapport often took years.

We observed too that many French firms were family affairs. When we bought "some very sweet early French novels" from Jammes, we were buying, not from the present generation, but from the father of the incumbents. Jammes Pere inclined to 17th-century French novels by Prechac or Bremond, and we delighted in the small octavo calf-bound volumes that traced *Le Procez de l'Amour* or *L'Amour à la Mode*. When the sons of the proprietor took over the establishment, both the estab- lishment and its stock would undergo a dramatic metamorphosis as the tastes of the younger firm members were manifested.

We have seen the same metamorphosis take place in other long- established Paris *librairies*. When we first ventured overseas for books, we dealt, for example, with Clavreuil Pere and with Chamonal Pere. As the years passed, the sons took over. And now, alas, we find that many of the sons have gone, replaced in France by their sons — the grandsons of those who started us on our way. It is cause for sadness at the same time that it is cause for rejoicing in the continuity of the French booktrade.

As time passed, we would continue our annual or semi-annual forays abroad, expanding our ports of call to other European nations as well as to the Orient. During the decades of travel that followed these early beginnings, however, we would add but few other mainstays to our overseas dramatis personae — our dear friends Bob and Emmy De Graaf of Holland come to mind. But we would not add many. In England and elsewhere we would continue to trade with those dealers whose geniality warmed us as their shelves intrigued us. We would continue, as long as we could, with those dealers who had become not only our sources of supply but an indispensable part of our lives.

The need and the love of books implies the need and the love of booksellers. They were — and, we add gratefully, they still are — inextricably bound one with the other.

INDEX

AB Bookman's Weekly, 23, 118
Ackermann, Rudolph, 46
Act against Unlicensed and
  Scandalous Books, An, 68
Alcaforada, Marianna, Letters of a
  Portuguese Nun, 69
Alcott, Louisa May, 2, 15, 70, 77, 139,
  157;
  Little Women, 70, 157
Alder, Antiquariat, 155
Aldine Press, 22, 24, 39, 40, 55, 128,
  140, 155;
  Venetian Academy, 60, 155
Allen, Edward G. & Son, Ltd., 10, 22,
  45, 46, 62
Allwoerden, Henricus de, 45, 46
American Revolution, 126
Amsterdam, Holland, 15, 42, 122, 136
Andreini, Isabella, 108
Andrieux, Librairie, 119, 120, 125, 145,
  163
Antiquarian Bookman, 109 see also AB
  Bookman's Weekly
Antiquarian Book Monthly Review, 1,
  57
Antiquarian Booksellers Association
  (England), 59–60, 84
Antiquarian Booksellers Association of
  America, 107, 111;
  Middle Atlantic Chapter, 118
Antwerp, Belgium, 10, 53
Aretino, Pietro, 129
Argences, Librairie d', 127
Armed Forces Medical Library, 144
Armstrong, Neville, 70
Art Ancien, L', 155
Atkins, Eileen, 46
Attlee, Clement, 99
Aubin, Nicolas, Histoire des Diables
  de Loudun, 93
Augsburg, Germany, 21
Austin, Texas, 39, 40

Austria As It Is (by Charles Sealsfield),
  131, 132

Bacon, Sir Francis, 55, 69;
  New Atlantis, 55, 161
Bader, Paul, 8, 156
Baer, E., 5, 44–45
Baer family, 44, 138
Baer, Leo, 44–45
Baker, Sidney, 120
Baldwin, Anne, 15, 84
Baldwin, Richard, 15, 83, 84, 156
Baluze, Etienne, 53
Barker, Margery, 106, 107
Barnard College, 2
Barnaud, Nicolas, 144
Barrett, Clifton Waller, 142
Basle, Switzerland, 14, 32, 81, 117,
  154–155, 156;
  University of, 83, 154–155
Beach, D.M., 133
Beaumont, William, Experiments and
  Observations on the Gastric Juice,
  10, 12, 62
Bebell, Clinton, 99
Beijers, J.L., 136
Bella, Stefano della, 96
Berne, Switzerland, 155, 156
Bernhardt, Sarah, Bibliotheque, 146
Bernstein, Michel, 5, 7, 125–126,
  143–144, 145, 160, 161–162
Bernstein, Monique, 144, 161
Berry, Donald, 62
Beze, Theodore de, 154;
  Icones, 100
Bibliographical Society (England),
  106
Bibliographical Society of America,
  Papers of the, 14, 74, 77, 84, 156
Bidloo, Govard, 53
Bishops Stortford, England, 60
Blackwell, B.H., Ltd., 44, 56, 69
Blackwood, Adam, 46
Blaricum, Holland, 123
Bloch, Joshua, 107
Blois, France, 143

Bloody Court, The, 68
Boccaccio, Giovanni, 136;
    Decameron, 21
Bocchi, Achille, 61, 62
Bodleian Library, 46, 69
Bodoni, Giambattista, 141
Boissat, Pierre, *Le Brillant de la*
    Royne, 100
Boleyn, Anne, 107
Bologna, Italy, 61, 62
Bondy, Louis W., 21
Bonivard, Francois de, 157
Book Fairs, 110, 118, 154
Booknoll Farm, 111
Boston Public Library, 77
Bowes & Bowes, 27
Boyle, Robert, 10, 11, 58, 62;
    Experiments And Considerations
        Touching Colours, 62, 129,
        130–131;
    library of, 11, 130–131;
    Sceptical Chemist, 130
Bremond, Gabriel de, 163
Breslauer, Bernard, 24, 54–55, 77
Breslauer, Martin, 54
Brighton, England, 53, 62
British Library, 57, 83, 142
Brown, Mrs. John Nicholas, 123
Browning, Elizabeth Barrett, 139;
    Poems, 57;
    Sonnets from the Portuguese, 57
Browning, Robert, 139, 143
Brunier, Librairie, 30, 31
Brussels, Belgium, 153, 154
Burgkmair, Hans, 21
Burke, J., 131, 132, 140
Burstein, E., Librairie Ancienne, 156
Byron, George Gordon, Lord, 67, 75,
    157

Caius, John, 27
Calais, France, 30, 86, 146
Calcagnini, Celio, *Opera*, 81
Calderwood, David, 72, 117
Callot, Jacques, 122, 123
Calvert, Phyllis, 47
Calvin, John, 56, 156, 158
Cambiagi, Gaetano, 140
Cambridge, England, 27, 37, 58, 75,
    106;

University, 58;
    Trinity College Library, 75
Cambridge, Massachusetts, 38
Campanella, Tommaso, *City of the*
    Sun, 55, 161
Campo, Antonio, 13, 107
Canterbury, England, 75–76;
    Cathedral, 76
Capella, Galeazzo Flavio, 160
Carwitham, John, 43
Cassini, Libreria, 137
Castaigne, Librairie, 153
Castlemaine, Roger, Earl of, 81
Catherine II, Empress of Russia, 100,
    122
Cavallotti, Dante, 69, 142, 143
Cavalotti, Signorina, 138
Cecchi, Gianmaria, 56, 142
Cellini, Benvenuto, *Vita*, 100
Chamonal, Francois et Rodolphe, 9,
    118–119, 125, 161
Chamonal, Pere, 8, 118, 146, 161, 163
Chamonix, France, 156, 157–158
Charlemagne, 100
Charles I, King of England, 154
Charles II, King of England, 68, 156
Charles V, H.R.E., 22
Chaucer, Geoffrey, 76, 84
Chicago, Illinois, 107
Chiesa, Carlo Alberto, 159
Churchill, Winston, 46, 75
Clark, William Andrews, Library, 71,
    72
Clavreuil, Bernard, 86, 96
Clavreuil, Jean, 86, 87, 96
Clavreuil, Librairie Historique, 9, 86,
    92, 93, 96, 117, 120, 125, 162
Clavreuil, Raymond, 9, 86–87, 96,
    162, 163
Cleopatra, Queen of Egypt, 24
Cochlaeus, Johann, 107
Coecke, Pieter, 53
Cohn, Louis Henry, 72
Cohn, Marguerite, 148
Coligny, Gaspard de, 144
Collis, Ruth, 98, 132
Colonna, Vittoria, 37, 45
Columbia University, 2, 55, 70, 148;
    Avery Architectural Library, 98, 148
Commin, H., 133

Index

Concord, Massachusetts, 70, 77
Congregation for the Propaganda of
    the Faith, 62
*Constitution de la Lune...Par le
    Cousin-Jacques* (by Louis Abel
    Beffroy de Regny), 126
Contarini, Gasparo, *Commonwealth
    and Government of Venice*, 128
Copernicus, Nikolaus, 81, 119
Copinger, H.B., 20–21, 37
Coppet, Andre de, 77
Cornell University Library, 12, 24, 132
Cosimo III, Grand Duke of Tuscany,
    100
Cousteau, Pierre, *Pegma*, 61, 96
Cracow, Poland, 144
Cranach, Lucas, 26
Cremona, Italy, 13, 107
Crichton, James, 55, 143
Cromwell, Oliver, 68
Cumberland Hotel, London, 4, 19, 48,
    59, 66, 72, 97, 98, 106, 112, 146
Curio, Coelius Secundus, 155
Cyrano de Bergerac, Savinien, 74

Danieli Hotel, Venice, 136, 137
Dante Alighieri, 138
Dasypodius, Cunradus, *Heron
    Mechanicus*, 70
David of Cremona, 107
Davis, Irving, 6, 9, 10, 23, 24, 29, 36,
    37, 38, 52, 53, 54, 55, 69–70, 98, 99,
    100, 101, 108, 110, 125, 129, 143, 145,
    147, 148
Davis & Orioli, 22, 29;
    Memoirs by Orioli, 132
Davy, Sir Humphry, *Description of the
    Safety Lamp*, 86
Dawson, William, 86, 132
De Graaf, Bob, 164
De Graaf, Emmy, 164
Deny, Librairie, 153, 154
Descartes, Rene, 12;
    Principes de la Philosophie, 11, 87,
    88
Desruelles, Librairie, 87
De Thou, Jacques-Auguste de, 21
Dibner, Bern, 70
Dickens, Charles, 6, 74, 142

Diderot, Denis, *Plan of the French
    Encyclopaedia*, 86;
    Lettre Sur Les Aveugles, 132
Disraeli, Benjamin, 83–84
Dobell, Percy, 26
Dolce, Lodovico, 142
Dolium Diogenis, 53
Domizlaff, Helmuth, 116
Dommergues, Librairie, 94
Doni, Antonio Francesco, *Libraria*,
    108;
    Disegno, 143
Donne, John, 74
Dorbon, Librairie, 94, 127, 163
Dore, Pierre, 120
Dover, England, 30, 86
Dring, Edmund, 6, 24, 58
Driscoll, Emily, 76–77, 98, 127
Dunton, John, *Religio Bibliopolae*, 77
Durtal, Chez, 119

Eck, Johann, 26
Edinburgh, Scotland, 85
Edwards, Francis, Ltd., 42, 43, 61,
    67–68
Edwards, Harold W., 8, 73, 101
Edwards, Olive, 73, 101
Eisemann, Heinrich, 30, 83
Eisenhower, Dwight D., 94
Elizabeth I, Queen of England, 46,
    75, 160
Elizabeth II, Queen of England, 43,
    134
Elizabeth, Queen Consort, 47
Elte, Max, 123, 152
Elte, Meier, 122, 123
Emmington Chinor, England, 99
Ephemera, 13, 32–33, 43, 83, 88–89,
    93, 94–95, 96, 152, 162
Erasmus, Desiderius, 32;
    Praise of Folly, 14, 32;
    Encomium Matrimonii, 32;
    Epistolae, 57;
    Querela Pacis, 148
Ercole in Tebe (by Giovanni Andrea
    Moniglia), 100
Erler, Mabel, 12
Eschlimann, Dr., 159
Estienne Family, 25
Estienne, Henri II, 11, 21, 110

Estienne, Robert, 22
Ettinghausen, Dr. Maurice, 44
Exeter, England, 133

Factum pour... U.G. Prestre, 93
Falconia Proba, Valeria, Centones, 124
Fall, John, 12
Fauchet, Claude, Eloge de Franklin,
    162
Feisenberger, H.A., 38–39, 40, 132
Feminism, 37, 55, 82, 93, 98, 108, 124,
    146, 159–160
Fernandes de Queiros, Pedro, 95;
    Copie de la Réqueste, 11, 94–95
Ficino, Marsilio, 136
Fiesole, Itali, 138
Fish, Simon, Supplication of the
    Beggars, The, 152
Fletcher, Constance, 25, 40
Fletcher, Ifan Kyrle, 25, 26, 40, 72, 73
Florence, Italy, 7, 24, 136, 137–140, 142
Florio, Michelangelo, 53
Folger Shakespeare Library, 12, 55, 77,
    83, 96, 111, 112, 114, 120, 128, 142,
    146, 147, 155, 156
Folkestone, England, 146
Fontana, Domenico, 19–20
Forset, Edward, Pedantivs, 37
Fournier, Pierre Simon, Manuel
    Typographique, 8, 146
Francis II, King of France, 96
Frankfurt A/M, Germany, 44, 110, 136;
    Book Fair, 11, 110
Franklin, Burt, 82
Frauendorfer, Dr., 155
French Revolution, 126, 144, 156–157,
    162
Froben, Jerome, 32
Froben, Johann, 22, 24, 32, 81
Fuller, Margaret, 77, 139
Fulton, Dr. John F., 131

Galanti, Baptiste, 145
Galilei, Galileo, 110, 139;
    Systema Cosmicvm, 110
Galle, Philippe, Imagines, 123
Galsworthy, John, Forsyte Saga, 58, 59
Geiler von Keysersberg, Johann,
    Nauicula penitentis, 21
Gelli, Giovanni Battista, 142

Geneva, Switzerland, 8, 155, 156, 157,
    158
George III, King of England, 57
George VI, King of Great Britain, 47
Gilhofer, Antiquariat, 114
Giraldi Cinthio, Giovanni Battista,
    56, 142;
    Hecatommithi, 39
Goering, Hermann, 52, 113
Goldschmidt, E.P., 6, 22–23, 24, 37,
    42, 43, 66, 71, 81, 97, 98, 109, 110,
    125, 128, 147, 148
Goldschmidt, Lucien, 69, 115
Gomme, Laurence, 114
Gonnelli, L., Libreria, 138
Gothier, Librairie, 153
Gozzini, Oreste, Libreria, 138
Grafton & Co., 8, 20–21, 22, 36, 37, 82,
    129, 147
Grandier, Urbain, 93
Grapheus, Cornelius, 157;
    Triumphe d'Anvers, 10, 52, 53
Grauer, Ben, 118
Greenwich, England, 148
Gregory, Katherine, 73
Grenailles, Francois de Chatonniere,
    Bibliotheqve des Dames, La, 146
Grey, Lady Jane, 53
Guildford, England, 45
Gurney, Richard D., 102, 103, 106, 107,
    128

Hague, The, Holland, 13, 32, 33, 122,
    136, 152
Hall, Joseph, Mundus Alter et Idem,
    55, 161
Hamel, Fanny, 8, 20, 21, 36, 37, 82, 129
Hamill, Frances, 106, 107, 114
Haraszti, Zoltan, 76, 77
Harding's, George, Bookshop, Ltd.,
    41, 42, 109, 129
Harper's, Miss, Bookstore, 133
Harris, Charles R., 42, 61, 68
Harvard University Library, 22, 36,
    38, 54, 70, 83, 146;
    Harvard Law Library, 21;
    Houghton Library, 38;
    Department of Printing and
        Graphic Arts, 38, 123
Harvey, William, 46

Index

Haus der Bücher (Erasmushaus), 14,
32, 154, 155
Havre, Le, France, 120
Hawthorne, Nathaniel, *Scarlet Letter*,
133
Heck, Antiquariat, 113, 114
Heffer & Sons, Ltd., 27
Hegenauer, Antiquariat, 155
Heitz, Paul, 71
Henry III, King of France and Poland,
144, 162
Henry IV, King of France, 145
Henry VIII, King of England, 28, 59,
99, 107, 108, 134
Herberstain, Sigismund, 102
Herrera, Juan de, 98
Hertzberger, Menno, 5, 122, 123, 155
Hierocles, 21
High Wycombe, England, 83, 84
Hildreth, Richard, *White Slave, The*,
138
Hill, Peter Murray, 47, 86,147, 149
Hilversum, Holland, 7, 11, 123, 124,
125, 127, 136, 152, 153
Hinterberger, Antiquariat, 8, 114
*Histoire Secrette de la Duchesse de
Portsmouth*, 156
Hoboken, New Jersey, 1, 3, 17, 33, 35,
50, 65, 135
Hodgson, Sydney, 74
Hoe, Robert, III, 146
Hoepli, Libreria Antiquaria, 141–142,
159
Hofer, Philip, 36, 38, 54, 123
Holbein, Hans, *Dance of Death*, 46
Holden, Miriam, 37, 82, 93, 99, 108
Hollar, Wenceslaus, 68
Holmes, Sherlock, 12–13, 14, 15, 68
Holocaust, 3, 5
Hooghe, Romein de, 53, 118
Hooke, Robert, 59
Hopewell, New Jersey, 111
Hotman, Francois, 124, 154;
Franco-Gallia, 124, 144
House of Books, Ltd., 72, 148
Hroswitha of Gandersheim, 108
Hutten, Ulrich, 57
Huxley, Aldous, *Devils of Loudun*, 93
Huysmans, Charles-Marie-Georges, 8;
Society, 119, 162

Imhoff, Georg Paulus,
Beschreibung...des Stück-Schiessen,
52–53, 54
Inman, Maurice, Inc., 98
Innocent XI, Pope, 82
Interlaken, Switzerland, 32
International Antiquariaat, 123
International League of Antiquarian
Booksellers, 112, 113, 123, 146–147;
1954Congress, 14, 107, 112–117, 120,
146;
1956 Congress, 5, 14, 146–149;
1967 Congress, 154;
1973 Congress, 118, 123
Isseido Booksellers, 118
Ithaca, New York, 132

Jackson, William A., 38
James II, King of England, 81
Jammes, Paul, Librairie, 162, 163
Janowitz, Dr. Henry, 62
Jepson, Mrs., 110
Joan of Arc, 97, 154
Joanereidos: Or, Feminine Valour (by
James Strong), 108
Jones, Inigo, 134
Joseph, Jack, 8, 46, 99, 118, 119, 131
Judaica, 13, 107, 145

Kant, Immanuel, *Zum Ewigen
Frieden*, 126
Kaye, Barbara (Muir), 60
Kaye, Thomas, 27
Kern, H.E., 122, 152
Kerr, Lord John, 127
Kettle's Paper Shop, 42
King, Raphael, 129
Kitzbühl, Austria, 117, 133
Knole House, 46
Knox, John, 158
Koch, Richard F., 117
Königsberg, Germany, 126
Kunreuther, Valerie, 18
Kup, Karl, 76, 77

*Labyrinthe Royal de L'Hercvle Gavlois
Triomphant* (by Andre Valladier),
145
Ladden, Nathan, 98, 101, 127, 128

La Harpe, Jean Francois, *Du Fanatisme Dans La Langue Revolutionnaire*, 156–157
Lambert, Pierre, 8, 119, 125, 162
Landi, Giulio, 24
Lang, Herbert, & Cie, 155
Languet, Hubert, 109, 154; *Vindiciae contra Tyrannos*, 109, 154
La Rochelle, France, 123
Larsen, Osbojrn Lungen, 115, 148
Laube, August, 155
Lechner, Antiquariat, 114
Le Clercq, Librairie, 153
Leconte, Librairie, 11, 87, 88, 127
Leeuwenhoek, Anthony van, 10, 58
Le Jeune de Boullencourt, *Description Generale de L'Hostel Royal des Invalides*, 87
Lenin, Nikolai, 112
Leo X, Pope, 82
Leslie, Mrs. Frank, 15, 39
Lettre D'Un Americain aux Citoyens Francois, Sur La Representation (by M. de La Chaise), 162
Leyden, Holland, 72
Library, The, 14–15, 147
Library of Congress, 83
Liege, Belgium, 153, 154
Lincoln, David, 44, 56, 69
Locke, John, *Treatise concerning Education*, 37
Lomazzo, Giovanni Paolo, 148; *Pittura*, 129
London, England, 3, 4, 5, 6, 10, 11, 14, 15, 16, 19, 20, 24, 27, 30, 31, 36, 37, 41, 43, 44, 48, 49, 50, 52, 53, 58, 60, 61, 62, 63, 66, 70, 71, 72, 73, 76, 77, 80, 82–83, 84, 85, 94, 97, 98, 99, 101, 106,107, 109, 111, 112, 117, 118, 120, 125, 127, 128, 129, 130, 131, 132, 140, 142, 145, 146, 147, 160;
Stationers' Hall, 15, 73, 74, 111, 131;
Somerset House, 15, 131;
School of Economics, 38;
Buckingham Palace, 50, 101;
St. Paul's Cathedral, 74, 111
Loock, van, Librairie, 153
Los Angeles, California, 71
Loudun, France, 93
Louis XIV, King of France, 87–88

Low, David, 25, 49, 99, 109; *With All Faults*, 99
Lutetia Hotel, Paris, 30, 97
Luther, Martin, 10, 25, 26, 31, 99, 107, 108, 114, 123, 155; *Sermon* (1519), 10, 26, 31
Lyon, H.D., 102, 103
Lyons, France, 156

Machiavelli, Niccolo, 56–57, 136, 139
Madliger, Antiquariat, 156
Maggs Bros., Ltd., 6, 9, 22, 23, 57, 73, 74, 82, 98, 103, 108, 142, 148
Maggs, Clifford, 1, 57, 82, 98, 108, 148
Magis, Jean-Jacques, 96–97, 117, 125, 162
Mallarmé, Stéphane, 157
Manet, Edouard, 157
Manutius, Aldus, the Younger, 55
Manuzio, Aldo, Libreria, 159
Marat, Jean Paul, *Chaines de L'Esclavage, Les*, 69
Marconville, Jean de, 145
Marks & Co., 26, 66–67, 99, 131
Marlowe, Christopher, *Tamburlaine*, 152
Martyn, John, 15, 59, 73, 74
Mary, Countess of Pembroke, 134
Mary, Queen of Scots, 46, 47, 126
Marzoli, Carla, 142, 143
Massey, Dudley, 77
Maximilian I, H.R.E., 148
Mazarinades, 125
McLeish & Sons, 20, 21, 36–37, 70, 86, 97, 108, 127, 128, 147
Medici, Catherine de, 21
Medici family, 7, 100, 119, 139, 140, 142
Medici, Francesco de, 139
Medici, Lorenzo the Magnificent, 139
Mediolanum, Libreria Antiquaria, 142, 143, 159
Melanchthon, Philip, 56
Memoirs of a Social Monster (by Charles Price), 128
Menage, Jelle, 5, 122
Metropolitan Museum of Art, 62, 100, 140
Michelangelo Buonarroti, 24, 37, 139
Miette, Librairie, 153
Milan, Italy, 136, 140, 141–143, 158–160

Index

Milstein, Nathan, 52
Milton, John, 69;
   Areopagitica, 68
Montpersan, Louis de, Politique des Jesuites, La, 130–131
Montreux, Switzerland, 157
Moorthamers, Louis, Librairie, 153
Morata, Olympia Fulvia, 53, 98
Morelli, Jacopo, Libreria di San Marco, 137
Morgan, Charles, 74–75
Moscow, Russia, 70, 100
Moxon, Joseph, 23
Muir, Percy, 59–60
Munich, Germany, 28, 93, 116, 124, 149, 161
Murmellius, Johannes, Versificatio, 23, 24
Myers, Winifred, 9, 47, 84–85, 100, 106, 107, 115–116, 143

Napoleon I, Emperor of France, 87, 127
Nebehay, Ingo, 114, 155
Neroni & Prandi, Libreria, 140–141
Neville, Peter, 70
Newberry Library, 12, 21, 24, 42, 83, 107, 142, 154
Newbury, England, 8, 101
New Orleans, Louisiana, 39, 40, 132
Newton, Sir Isaac, 10, 58;
   Opticks, 108
New York, N.Y., 2, 18, 39, 44, 47, 48, 61, 110, 141, 142, 146, 154, 157, 158
New York Public Library, 12, 43, 55, 77;
   Spencer Collection, 77;
   Jewish Division, 107
New York University, 2
Niemyer, Elizabeth, 112
Nijhoff, Martinus, 13, 32, 33, 122, 125, 136, 152
Nobele, F. de, Librairie, 92
Norman, Francis, 4, 8, 11, 43–44, 71–72, 80–81, 119, 130–131, 149, 155
North Georgia Gazette, 7, 153
Nuremberg, Germany, 18, 54

Oesterreich über Alles (by Philipp Wilhelm von Hornick), 114

Ogilby, John, 68
Olivier, Sir Laurence, 40
Olschki, Cesare, 7, 137–138, 140
Olschki family, 138
Olschki, Leo S., Libreria, 137–138
Orleans, France, 126
Oxford, England, 27, 44, 56, 58, 68–69, 99;
   University, 58

Paget, William, 67
Pargellis, Stanley, 24
Paris, France, 5, 6, 7, 8, 9, 11, 13, 15, 16, 30–31, 45, 86, 87, 89, 92, 93–94, 95, 97, 101, 117, 120, 125, 127, 143, 144, 145, 146, 156, 159, 160, 161, 162–163;
   University of, 25
Parker, Theodore, 139
Parsons, Edward Alexander, 39;
   Bibliotheca Parsoniana, 39;
   Wonder and the glory, The, 39
Pascal, Blaise, 132
Payne, Alfred, 108
Payne, Carola, 95, 108
   see also Wormser, Carola Payne
Peddie, Robert A., 21, 36, 37
Pembroke family, 134;
   Wilton, 134
Perrault, Charles, Hommes Illustres, Les, 128
Perre, Francine van der, 153
Perre, van der, Librairie, 153, 154
Petit, Pierre, 93
Petitot, Librairie, 163
Petrarch, Francesco, 55
Pforzheimer, Arthur, 76
Pforzheimer, Carl H., 67
Pforzheimer, Carl H., Jr., 69
Philip II, King of Spain, 10, 53, 73, 98, 122;
   Index Librorum prohibitorum, 73
Piantanida, Sandro, 160
Picard, A., Librairie, 11, 92, 94, 120
Piccolomini, Aeneas Sylvius (Pope Pius II), 45
Pickering & Chatto, 77
Pico della Mirandola, Giovanni, 11, 12, 24, 125
Pico della Mirandola, Giovanni Francesco, 143

Pilgrim Press, 72, 117
Pirckheimer, Willibald, 120
Pisa, Italy, 67
Pitcher, Eleanor ("Molly"), 12, 111–112, 114, 120, 128, 133, 146, 147
Plummer, George, 131
Poccianti, Michele, *Catalogvs Scriptorvm Florentinorvm*, 136
Poe, Edgar Allan, 157
Pole, Reginald, Cardinal, 149
Police et Reiglement...des Pauvres de...Paris (by Jean Martin), 144
Polifilo, Il, Libri Rari, 142, 143
Porzio, Simone, 159
Postl, Karl Anton, 132; *see also* Sealsfield, Charles
Postwar Conditions, passim
Poullain de la Barre, François, *De L'Excellence des Hommes*, 93
Powell, Lawrence Clark, 70, 71, 72
Pozzi, Elfo, 142, 143, 159
Prague, Austro-Hungary, 132
Prandi, Dino, 140–141
Prandi, Gastone, 140–141
Prandi, Paolo, 140–141
Prechac, Jean de, 163
Prentis, Edmund, 20
Prestwick, Scotland, 106
Price, John, *Historiae Brytanicae Defensio*, 55
Priestley, Joseph, *Experiments...on Different Kinds of Air*, 132
Princeton University, 82
Providence, Rhode Island, 123

Quaritch, Bernard, Ltd., 6, 9, 10, 22, 23, 24, 58, 101

Rabelais, François, 145
Radaeli, Signora, 141, 159
Random House, 70
Rauch, Librairie, 157
Ravenna, Italy, 67
Ray, John, 10, 58; *Travels*, 23
Redgrave, Vanessa, 46
Reggio Emilia, Italy, 140
Reichmann, Felix, 12, 24, 132
Reichner, Herbert, 2, 44, 81, 125;

ed. *Philobiblon*, 81
Ricchi, Agostino, *Tre Tiranni*, 22
Ritter, François, 31
Rizzi, Renzo, 142, 143
Robertson, Keith, 111, 114
Roosevelt, Franklin Delano, 28, 37
Rosenberg, Ethel and Julius, 5, 97
Rosenthal, A., Ltd., 44
Rosenthal, Edith, 124
Rosenthal family, 138
Rosenthal, Hilde, 5, 7, 11, 123–125, 126, 136, 148, 152
Rosenthal, Jacques, 93
Rosenthal's, Ludwig, Antiquariaat, 7, 123, 124
Rostenberg, Leona, 23, 31, 38, 39, 44, 49, 55, 57, 61, 69, 71, 74, 76, 77, 81, 83, 84, 115, 126, 128, 132, 134, 140, 159, 161;
undergraduate and graduate studies, 2, 13;
apprenticeship, 2;
studies of 16th- and 17th-century English printer-publishers, 2, 14–15, 73, 84, 111, 131, 147, 156;
research in Strasbourg, 2, 21, 31, 70;
"John Martyn, 'Printer to the Royal Society,'" 15, 59, 73, 74;
"Richard and Anne Baldwin, Whig Patriot Publishers," 15, 84, 156;
"Robert Scott, Restoration Stationer and Importer," 15, 77;
"Nathaniel Thompson, Catholic Printer and Publisher of the Restoration," 15, 106, 147–148;
"Robert Stephens, Messenger of the Press," 15;
"John Bellamy: 'Pilgrim' Publisher of London," 15;
"Nathaniel Butter and Nicholas Bourne, First 'Masters of the Staple,'" 15;
Literary, Political, Scientific ... Publishing, Printing & Bookselling in England, 1551-1700: Twelve Studies, 15, 59, 74, 77, 84, 148;

Index

Library of Robert Hooke, The, 59;
"Tribute to E.P. Goldschmidt,"
109
Rostenberg, Leona - Rare Books, 3,
38, 87, 111, 116, 117–118;
Tenth Anniversary, 14, 117–118;
One Hundred Years of France 1547-
1652: A Documentary History
(Catalogue 34), 33, 88
Rostenberg & Stern, passim;
Old and Rare, 1, 13, 21, 31, 43, 57,
62, 119, 126, 145;
catalogues, 3, 25, 26, 54, 88, 108,
140;
collections, 7, 88–89, 140;
Quest Book - Guest Book, 14, 32
Rotterdam, Holland, 33, 35, 50, 51, 122,
135
Rousseau, Jean-Jacques, 114
Roux-Devillas, Francis, 13, 89, 92, 93
Royal Society, 59, 74;
Philosophical Transactions, 10,
58–59, 68
Ruexner, Georg, Thurnier-Buch, 114

Sabine, Sir Edward, ed., North
Georgia Gazette, 153
Sacher Hotel, Vienna, 112
Sack, Henri, 157
Sackville West family, 46
Safire, William, 157
Salem, Massachusetts, 93
Salisbury, England, 133
Salmon, William, Polygraphice, 86
Sandford, Francis, 81;
History of the Coronation
of...James II, 81
Savonarola, Girolamo, 47, 138
Scamozzi, Vincenzo, 110
Scaramouche, Vie de (by Angelo
Constantini), 128
Scarini, Silvestre, 69
Scheler, Lucien, 7, 96, 125
Schumann, Helmutt, 155
Schweitzer, Dr. Albert, 52
Scott, Robert, 15, 77;
Catalogus Librorum, 77
Scribe Hotel, Paris, 86, 117, 161, 163
Sealsfield, Charles, 132;
see also Postl, Karl Anton

Seebass, Dr., 32, 154, 155
Seligman, Ernst, 25–26, 31, 81, 99, 129
Servetus, Michael, 45, 46
Sforza, Isabella, 24, 45
Sforza, Massimiano, 107
Sgattoni, Libreria, 159
Shakespeare, William, 39, 53, 55, 128,
133, 134;
Merry Wives of Windsor, 55;
Othello, 39, 128
Shelley, Percy Bysshe, 13, 67, 109;
"Skylark," 67;
"Witch of Atlas," 67
Sidney, Sir Philip, 85, 134;
Arcadia, 134
Slatkine, Alexandre, 156, 157
Slatkine, Michel, 156, 157
Smith, Joseph, 56–57
Soldat François, 32
Sotheby & Company, 128, 147, 148
Southampton, England, 1, 3, 19, 65
Speroni, Sperone, 142
Spierinck, Nicolas, 27
Spinoza, Benedictus de, 42;
Tractatus Theologico-Politicus,
41–42, 102
Stalin, Joseph, 112
Stationers Company, 73
Steele, Geoffrey, 113
Stern, Isaac, 52
Stern, Madeleine, 38, 39, 44, 57, 62,
70, 75, 77, 84, 110, 115, 117, 128, 157;
undergraduate and graduate stud-
ies, 2, 13;
Guggenheim Fellowship, 2;
Louisa May Alcott, 2, 15, 70, 84;
Purple Passage: The Life of Mrs.
Frank Leslie, 15, 39;
Sherlock Holmes: Rare Book
Collector, 15;
Imprints on History: Book
Publishers and American
Frontiers, 15;
"Reminiscences of Book Buying
in England - 1947," 23;
Life of Margaret Fuller, The, 77;
and first New York Antiquarian
Book Fair, 110;
entry into Rostenberg firm, 117;
first trip abroad, 157

Stevens, B.F., & Brown, Ltd., 84, 98, 132
Stonehenge, 134
Strasbourg, France, 11, 21, 31, 70, 71, 125, 154, 161;
  University of, 2;
  Cathedral, 31, 48, 161
Strawberry Hill, 106, 107
Stroheim, Erich von, 52
Sydney, Cape Breton Island, 106
Sylvius: *see* Piccolomini

Tagliente, Giovanni Antonio, 73
Takeley, England, 60
Tamerlane the Great, 7, 152
Tapisseries du Roy, 85
Thiebaud, J., 8, 86, 87, 94, 117
Thomas-Scheler, Librairie, 9, 96
Thorp, Thomas, 19–20, 45, 97, 128
Tokyo, Japan, 118, 123
Traylen, Charles W., 45, 46
Trissino, Giovanni Giorgio, 142
Tryal of Nathanael Thompson, 147–148
Tulkens, Florian, 154

Ubaldini, Petruccio, 82, 100
University of Basle Library, 154, 155
University of Illinois, 60, 142
University of Kansas, 69, 108
University of Oklahoma Press, 70
University of Sydney, 148
University of Texas, 39
University of Toronto, 142
Utrecht, Holland, 136

Varchi, Benedetto, 29, 136
Vasari, Giorgio, 24;
  Lives of the Artists, 24, 37
Vellekoop, Jacques, 23, 71, 98, 109, 127, 128, 147, 148
Venice, Italy, 47, 55, 57, 136–137, 142, 143
Vevey, Switzerland, 157
Victoria, Queen of England, 83
Vidal-Maigret, Mme., 145–146
Vienna, Austria,5, 8, 14, 15, 67, 81, 107, 112–117, 120, 132, 146, 148
Vieri, Francesco de, 55
Vigevani, Alberto, 142, 143

Vilna, Russia, 148
Vinci, Leonardo da, 37, 72, 107, 139, 142, 143
Vinciana, Libreria, 159, 160
Vita & Virginia (by Eileen Atkins), 46
Vivien et Beurlet, 92–93
Voirol & Cie, 155, 156

Walpole, Horace, 106
Washington, D.C., 111
Weil, Ernest, 6, 11, 28, 47, 67, 71, 76, 81, 82, 110, 114, 128, 129, 149
Wells, William Charles, *Essay on Dew*, 86
Wepf, Antiquariat, 154
Westward Ho!, England, 133
Wheeler, Stanley G., 41, 42, 109–110, 129
White, George W., 60–61
Wilkins, John, *Monde Dans La Lune, Le*, 128
William III, King of England, 52, 53
Willughby, Francis, 58
Wing, Donald G., 12, 24, 70, 72;
  STC of English Books 1640-1700, 70, 71, 72
Wolfe, John, 129
Woodburn, Elisabeth (Mrs. Keith Robertson), 110, 111, 114
Woolacombe, England, 133
World War II, 9, 18, 53, 126, 161;
  effects of, passim
Wormser, Carola Payne, 106, 108;
  see also Payne, Carola
Wormser, Richard S., 106, 107–108
Worstel-Konst (by Nicolaes Petter), 118
Wren, Christopher, 58
Wright, Michael, *Account of ... Castlemaine's Embassy*, 81–82

Yale Medical Library, 100, 131
Yale University Library, 12, 24, 83

Zenger, John Peter, *Trial of*, 86
Zurich, Switzerland, 112, 155, 156

LEONA ROSTENBERG founded Leona Rostenberg–Rare Books in New York City in 1944, and was joined by Madeleine Stern in 1945. Since then the two have been partners in the firm, now known as Rostenberg and Stern. Leona is past-president of the Antiquarian Booksellers Association of America, and past-delegate to the International League of Antiquarian Booksellers. She holds a Ph.D. in History from Columbia University. She is also the author of works on 17th-century English printing and publishing.

MADELEINE STERN is past-governor of the Antiquarian Booksellers Association of America, organizer of the first antiquarian book fair in America, and a founder of the Antiquarian Booksellers Center. She is also the author of biographies of Margaret Fuller, Louisa May Alcott, and Mrs. Frank Leslie, as well as numerous books on 19th-century American publishing history and feminism. A former Guggenheim Fellow, she has written and edited several works concerned with her particular interest, the life and writings of Louisa May Alcott.

Leona Rostenberg and Madeleine Stern are currently at work on a joint autobiography.